A Copper in Castleford

A Copper in Castleford

Tales Of A Bobby's Adventurous Life

Robin Whatley

authorHOUSE®

AuthorHouse™ UK Ltd.
1663 Liberty Drive
Bloomington, IN 47403 USA
www.authorhouse.co.uk
Phone: 0800.197.4150

Published by AuthorHouse   08/14/2013

ISBN: 978-1-4918-7557-5 (sc)
ISBN: 978-1-4918-7558-2 (e)

Contents

Chapter 1
No Windows

A corrugated asbestos shed, three-quarters of a mile long. And no windows.

That was my workplace. It was called the new section and was attached to a red-brick engineering workshop.

The shed housed a sheet metal working department, a profile burning area where heavy steel sheets were cut to shape and size, a plater's area where, working from blueprints, men welded the cut pieces together, and finally a semi-automatic welders' area, where men did the final welding before the gargantuan pieces passed out of the shed and into the main workshop, where they were machined, fitted with motors and hydraulics, painted and badged—and went out as heavy sheet metal working machines for pressing, folding and forming all manner of things to keep the world turning.

The shed was a lively place. An overhead crane rolled backwards and forwards, moving materials and the machines about, and there was the constant sound of metal being beaten, ground and welded.

And there were no windows.

Not that there was any scenery to be seen, since the shed stood alongside the Wakefield-York main railway line and a black-stained river.

The son of a male nurse and a tailoress, and the grandson of miners on both sides of the family, I was twenty-two years old, a plater, and newly married. We had just discovered that my wife was pregnant. She and I were excited and nervous and overjoyed all at once. I had no worries. I had a skilled job and was well paid, and we had a small mortgage, but we calculated that with a little overtime at work, which was always to be had. We would manage, and my wife would be able to stop work and raise our child.

Then two things happened that would change my life.

"Did you see that snowstorm this afternoon? It was a proper blizzard." This was an innocent remark my wife made as we were settling down to an evening of watching the telly, I'll never, ever forget that telly. It was a 20-inch colour Ferguson, reconditioned from Radio Rentals.

How could I see a snowstorm? The shed had no windows and the snow hadn't settled, so when I left for home I was unaware of any snowstorm.

Two weeks later the management called a general meeting during our dinner break—they took a bit of liberty there—but we all gathered, a hundred or so skilled workers, semi-skilled workers and labourers in the shed (with no windows). We were informed that the company's sales were at a record high and that the order books were full; our futures were secure. But our union colleagues, the power workers who manned the power stations, were in dispute over pay and conditions and were working to rule. So not working overtime to keep everything working and running smoothly, and as a result power output was reduced.

"What has this to do with us?" was the question on many lips. Then we found out that the government had decided to ration electricity to industrial units in order to lessen the effect on the general public, so we were to have power in our workshops on Mondays, Tuesdays and Wednesdays. At that time, Saturday morning was part of our working week, so beginning the next day, we were reduced to a three-day week and half-pay at a single stroke. The only consolation was that we would receive dole money for the remainder of the week.

To receive this payment, we had to queue outside of the foreman's office at the end of our shift on Wednesday afternoon and see the Unemployment Office staff which management had brought in.

I signed my name, took the little brown envelope, went back to my workbench and sat where I took my lunch every day, in the shed with no windows. I opened the envelope to discover my fate.

I had received three pounds.

Chapter 2
A New Job

My mind was in a whirl. What would I tell my newly pregnant wife? I had a mortgage to pay, bills to pay and food to buy—and now my wage was reduced by half. The union dispute was predicted to last for months.

How had I gotten here? I was raised on a council estate and had failed my eleven-plus, so I was to receive only a secondary education. I left school at fifteen and went to work as a panel beater/welder in a couple of local garages. At the same time, I attended a technical college on day release and night school until I obtained my welding certificates. A move to a boilermaking company gave me more experience in heavy engineering, and then a qualification in technical drawing gave me the chance to work as a plater—you guessed it, in the shed.

Weeks passed. I thought day and night about our future until I saw a national newspaper advertisement for prison officers. I had a eureka moment. This was the perfect answer: full-time work, security, regular hours, regular pay. Perfect. I applied for the forms straight away. I knew a friend of a friend who was in the prison

4

service, so I arranged to see him to try to get some idea of what the job would be like.

What a disappointment it was when I sat and listened to him say that his only complaint about working in a prison was the lack of—you guessed it again—windows.

I reckoned being locked up with criminals all day when I had not committed any crime would not be a good thing for me.

I had another eureka moment and answered another advertisement, this time for the police force.

I was granted an interview with a constable from my local police station, Castleford. We chatted for a while, and the more I learned, the more I liked the idea of being a policeman.

I was given a general knowledge exam, a physical exam and a more formal interview at the Wakefield Headquarters, and then I was accepted.

My life had changed in a way in which I was yet unaware. It was April 1973 when I attended the West Yorkshire Constabulary Training School, Bishopgarth, in Wakefield.

On day one, the first order of business was a haircut. The mod-style cut I had paid a fortune for just so I could look like one of the Small Faces pop group, soon lay on the floor, mingling with the shorn locks of about thirty others.

Next it was time to be fitted for a uniform. We new policemen were carefully measured before we were given uniforms that didn't fit. After trying many more tunics and trousers, suddenly we were all transformed and looked smart—like peas in a pod!

Then we moved into a classroom where, for the next two weeks, we were taught how to wear the uniform, how to complete a pocket notebook—which becomes the diary of every detail of your working day—and, most important, how to recognise the badges of rank within the police. This was so that if an officer screamed, "Jump!" you could look at his rank and then know instantly just how high you needed to jump.

Once a day we were taken outdoors and taught how to walk in unison. Our trainers told us that this was called marching. Judging from the obvious enthusiasm the drill instructor had for this style of walking, it was clearly a very important part of being a police officer, so much so that when we got it wrong, the poor chap went bright red and screamed abuse at us.

He was a nice chap, but he did scream a lot. I wondered if he owned a dog and, if he did, if—when it was time for walkies—he would scream, "By the left, quick march!" at the poor creature.

CHAPTER 3

Training School

The first two weeks of training were over, and I enjoyed a long weekend at home before we were dispatched to a regional police training centre.

I was the first person in my family or circle of friends who had become a policeman, so everyone I encountered in my home town was interested in what I had learned and what I could do. I stuck out my chest, raised to my full height of six-foot-one and announced that I could now dress myself, complete a diary and walk properly! The weekend flew past.

On Monday morning at Bishopgarth, the other new coppers and I were loaded onto the force coach and bussed northwards to Pannal Ash Police Training Centre on the outskirts of Harrogate.

Spirits were high on the coach. Someone at the back hummed a little. Before we knew it, we had arrived.

Before the coach came to a complete halt, the door was thrown open and a uniformed sergeant with a gleaming peak to his flat hat and with boots to match leaped into our lives. We came to know him affectionately as the drill pig. This man was the drill instructor and martial arts expert who, in the next twelve weeks, would disfigure our minds and bodies and make men of us— the two policewomen, as well.

I never found out who had upset him, but it was overly obvious that just before he got on our coach, someone had really pissed him off. He was fuming. He had a short piece of wood under his arm which he grasped tightly and then used a bit like a magic wand to detect which of us needed another haircut. He called the wand his pace stick. I later found out that all drill pigs carried one and that they were not used only to detect long hair. The drill pig walked down the coach's centre aisle in the manner that I now knew as marching. He turned and headed back to the front, which is when he pointed his wand at our heads as he passed and screamed, "Haircut!" to each one of us.

I knew he was unhappy because just before he left the coach, he announced that we were all scruffy bastards and had to parade at 7 p.m. sharp—number one ablutions—or else.

We had to find a calmer member of the training staff to interpret his words, which meant that we had to go to ("parade") in the washroom ("ablutions") designated number one at seven o'clock that evening or else we would suffer serious abuse or injuries—or worse.

Once we got off of the coach, we were introduced to our quarters, which in my case was a bedroom with eight beds, eight wardrobes and a large table covered with a blanket on which we could iron our uniforms. There were four irons, so I guessed that ironing was pretty important to our captors—sorry, instructors.

We had an en—suite with eight washbasins and four baths.

Then we were in the classroom for most of the rest of the day, where we were re-informed how to wear the uniform and complete our pocketbooks. Next, we went outside for a spell to be taught the walking bit all over again. The drill pig had calmed down a little by this time, but every now and then he would look closely at one of us, shake his head and shudder.

By this time we had been split up from our original group and were formed into classes of recruits from police forces from all over the north of England and Newcastle (Newcastle is that independent state in the north, not connected to the rest of the country).

After class, we were sent to our dormitories to change into our best uniforms, which we had to iron first. We then had to iron the other uniforms we had worn in class. Following this, we had to iron our third uniforms so that we had a spare, just in case. (No one explained in case of what, and none of us had the bottle to question this, so we just passed an hour or so pressing heavy serge uniforms that were covered with pleats, buttons, pockets and other obstacles designed to confuse a person who had never ever ironed anything before in his life, except for the odd hankie).

Then it was into the dining room for the evening meal. Good food was thrown onto our plates, but what the hey, we could always sponge down and iron the tunics again before we went to bed.

Finally, 7 p.m. loomed in our lives. About eighty of us shuffled into number one ablutions, which was the biggest ablutions with row after row of washbasins.

We waited, and we waited. A few thought about sneaking away but then remembered jolly old Drill Pig and decided that they needed a haircut anyway.

He arrived. The hairdresser was in his eighties, was short-sighted, and had been banned from practising in public because of the number of injuries he had inflicted onto other people's heads. He walked straight into the first row of washbasins and cursed. He apologised when he realised we were there. A chair was produced, and the first trembling victim was ushered to sit down. The hairdresser removed his glasses and went to work using only the sense of touch. I'm sure that first lad passed out, as he had to be helped away, it had all been too much for his nerves. I felt at my two-week growth and went next. They say the difference between a bad haircut and a good one is only a week. None of us had gotten to go home for the first four weeks, but once we were granted leave and I visited home, my wife cried when she saw my hair. When I went into the local pub for a pint, people's reaction to my haircut was opposite: the place went into an uproar.

During the twelve weeks of the training course, you get two long weekends at home. On one of these weekends I went into Castleford to do some shopping and bumped into the police constable (PC) who had visited me at home and gave me my first interview. He was walking around the town centre with the chief inspector (C.I), about whom I will say plenty later. The C.I's name was Gusscott, and he was an awesome man with a deep Cornish accent. He showed an interest in how I was getting on at training school and then went off saying what a wonderful place Castleford was for a young copper to start out. The variety of work was ideal to give a new recruit just the right start, he said. Why, only last week someone had nicked the Sea Cadets' barge and sailed it farther along the canal, so Castleford had its first case of piracy, he informed me. I took it all in until I saw the twinkle in his eye.

My being married and owning my own home in Castleford, it was very unlikely that I would be posted there. Upon hearing this, Gusscott lost interest, mumbled something and walked off.

Back at training, we discovered that there was a bar on-site—a wooden hut named the Red Lion. It was basically our social club, and when I say basic, I mean basic. There was a pool table, a skittles game and bingo. Every evening, one or two of the course instructors would drink there in order to keep an eye on us. Anyone seen to be drinking a few too many was elected to call the next game of bingo, which could be hilarious.

CHAPTER 4
The Great Escape

A couple of us discovered that there was another place of refreshment a few miles beyond our perimeter fence. This pub was in a very quiet country location and featured a very buxom barmaid. The name was the Squinting Cat—the pub's name, not the barmaid's!

There was only one problem. Some of our predecessors had been there and caused a scandal that was not talked about. And the place was strictly out of bounds.

Four of us formed an escape committee and formulated a cunning plan.

We found that the nearest point to our goal was a wire fence behind the greenhouses which produced some of the food for our table. Beyond the fence was a ditch filled with stagnant water, and beyond that were a couple of fields containing cattle. Once we navigated through that area, a brisk walk along a mile or so of tarmac road would take us there, or at least that was the plan.

During our dinner break, Bill from Pontefract, Steve from Rotherham, Will from Barnsley and I would wander off around the grounds in different directions and then cunningly meet behind the greenhouses. We found a joint in the wire fence and carefully unjoined it in such a way that a casually observing eye would not notice that it had been tampered with. Next, we found an old plank of wood to serve as a bridge over the stinking ditch.

All was in place and ready for what would become known as the Great Escape.

We set about to choosing a suitable night to make our way to the Squinting Cat. We determined that the venue should be fairly busy so we could remain unnoticed but that we should not go on a night when some of our instructors were likely to be there. We deliberated for hours and finally chose a night when there was to be some function—a birthday or something—in the officers' mess.

All of us met in the Red Lion and then quietly left one by one. We formed our little team behind the greenhouses and then slipped through the fence, over the bridge, across the fields and down the road—and then we were there. It worked like clockwork. With every round of drinks we finished, we patted ourselves on the back and bought more beer.

In no time at all, the pub was closing. We took one last, longing look at the barmaid's delights and left to make our way back.

I must point out that at this time we were drunk—rolling drunk, with not a care in the world.

Despite that it was now pitch-black, we found the farmer's gate, got through it and—being responsible people, officers of the law, no less—spent the next thirty minutes making sure that the gate was secured behind us. Then off we went. Earlier in the evening, none of us had noticed the prolific amount of cow shit there was in those two fields, but now we discovered just about every pile. We hopped and stumbled, slipped and slid, our way to the ditch.

Will was last to walk the plank. We who had crossed first stood and watched in some merriment as he started to lose his balance. Then, following a mighty crack, the plank broke, and Will dropped gracefully into the ditch. Being a team, we three who had crossed first grabbed some part of Will and pulled as hard as we could, at first without success. Shortly, and accompanied by an enormous sucking noise, Will was projected to safety. However, unable to stop himself, he smashed straight through the end wall of a greenhouse.

By some kind of miracle, Will was unhurt, although he was missing a shoe. We waited a while to make sure the coast was clear and that no one had heard the noise. When we walked down along the greenhouses, we came for the first time into a lit area. I took a glance at Will. He was covered in cow shit, green slime and dozens of squashed tomatoes. We all had a little giggle and scraped him down as best we could before retiring to our beds.

The next day the news broke that burglars had broken into our greenhouses and had stolen a quantity of fresh tomatoes. The very cheek of it, breaking into a police training centre!

There were other amusing incidents at Pannal Ash, but first you must realise that the recruits were all between nineteen, the youngest qualifying age, and thirty, the oldest (unless you came from the Armed Forces, in which case the upper age limit was thirty-two). We were adults, male and females all together, miles from home, miles from our loved ones, with Home Office subsidised beer prices. In other words, there was very cheap booze and lots of 'you know what' for those who required such things. Since I was from a decent, upright family and had a heavily pregnant wife who would have castrated me if I had so much as thought of straying from the path of decency, I settled for the cheap beer.

I have already mentioned the drill pig. He was a sergeant, as were the rest of the instructors. They took it in turns to be night duty sergeant.

One night the drill pig, affectionately known as Pig, was doing his rounds as night duty sergeant when he heard scuffling and giggling coming from a darkened classroom. He bravely opened the door, put on the light and disturbed a male recruit who came from Huddersfield and a female recruit who came from Nottingham—both of whom shall remain nameless. The couple was on a desk in a very passionate position.

Drill Pig screamed (he was incapable of normal-volume speech) something that would have really worried his mother: "[Nameless recruit] from Huddersfield, what the f*   * *g h**l are you doing?"

The recruit replied, "Just necking, Sarge."

The pig screamed, "Well, my son, put your neck back in your trousers and give me twenty-five laps of the parade ground at the double, now." We never discovered just what punishment Nameless from Nottingham received!

One night of gay abandon (*gay* in those days meant being of a happy and light-hearted disposition), I and a few others strolled through the main gates to visit the local pub, the Greyhound. This hostelry was not out of bounds, and we soon found out why. It was empty of customers, and the beer was lukewarm and flat. Even the locals shunned it.

So on the way back to confinement I decided to cheer up the other chaps by having a bit of a lark. When we passed through the main gates, I threw myself down on the immaculately groomed grass verge, grasped the picket fence with my arms and legs, and started to crawl on my side along the fence while at the same time shouting that I would be glad to get to the top of this ladder. No one laughed, which I thought odd. Then I looked up to see Chief Superintendent P., the centre's commandant, walking his poodle before turning in. He was not laughing either, so I thought I'd better leg it, which I did. I got away with my hijinks for exactly eight hours. The next morning we had a kit inspection before breakfast, which included an inspection of our wardrobes. I found it hard to believe that I was the only one whose shirt and jeans were grass-stained. Now that's what I call unlucky.

CHAPTER 5

Unharmed Combat

We were informed that some members of the public did not exactly like the police and that some of them, in fact, actually resented us so much that they responded with physical violence to our kindly approaches.

The solution to this problem was to give us even more training. Now getting dressed, keeping a diary and walking properly was not enough; we were to be trained in self-defence and then taught how to arrest and detain people who really didn't want to be arrested and detained—and who didn't want to discuss it in a friendly manner.

This is where things got physical with our friendly drill pig, who now was the martial arts instructor about to realise his fondest dreams of getting his hands on us and screaming abuse at the same time.

Previously we had never looked closely at our pig, mostly because of his bad breath that was hard to avoid when he was screaming in your face, and partly because the peak of his cap came down over his eyes. Now he was dressed in a kind of pair of white pyjamas with a black belt tied in the middle. No shoes, no socks and no hat.

He gave us a funny Japanese name for what we were about to learn, but we all forgot it and so called it Smackemandnickem.

We wore our gym gear. For the men, this consisted of vests and shorts; for the women, T-shirts and shorts. The men trained with men, and the women with women, so as to avoid the accidental grabbing of bits and pieces that the pig didn't want us to grab. Funny, he was the one wearing pyjamas!

We did a lot of grabbing and pulling and tripping up and arm-twisting and kneecap kicking until we were bored, so Pig introduced us to how to throw each other overhead. My partner was a whingeing little shit from Bradford. At this time, Bradford was a separate force from West Yorkshire and hence was our closest rival.

Bradford City Police height requirements were much less than ours were, so this guy was only five feet two inches tall, almost a foot shorter than I. When he tried to get me off balance and throw me over his shoulder, I just planted my feet. No matter how he wriggled and tugged, he could not get me airborne, so he announced, "Sarge, he won't let me throw him." Pig decided to give everyone a demonstration, and before I knew what was happening I was very definitely airborne with such velocity that I remained inverted until I made contact with the ground, head first.

I awoke looking up at a white ceiling and noticing the delicate scent of disinfectant and iodine. I was in the matron's room with a pain in the neck—not her, it was an actual pain in my neck. Next stop was Harrogate General Infirmary for x-rays and the fitting of a neck brace to support my torn muscles.

Was I resentful? Not one bit. For the last two weeks of training I was excused uniform, which meant that I no longer had to walk in unison, iron my uniforms or engage in Smackemandnickem.

And better yet—wait for this—every time I met Pig, he no longer screamed at me. Even better still—you won't believe this—every time I met him in the Red Lion, he bought me a pint of beer! Unbelievable, I know, but true.

The neck was better after a couple of days, but the matron, God bless her wrinkly socks, said, "Better safe than sorry," so the brace remained on until the end of the course. Was I going to argue?

On the very last day, when we were all in civvies anyway, I took off the brace and got everyone to sign it, all except that little shit from Bradford. When I invited the pig to sign it, he went very, very red and started screaming again. Strange.

So there we were, properly dressed and everything, with our heads buzzing with newly learned law. We paraded for the last time and were given our postings. Because of shortages in manpower there, I was posted to Castleford, the very place I didn't expect, along with three new mates.

CHAPTER 6
Castleford

Situated in West Yorkshire in the heart of the mining area, Castleford, better known locally as Cas, had four deep mines, a glassworks, two chemical works, three tailoring factories, a flour mill, a malt-roasting company and dozens of engineering workshops that made all manner of things from steam boilers to glass bottle moulds.

Cas stood on two main rail lines, the Leeds-York and the Wakefield-York. On the outskirts of the town centre, the River Aire and the River Calder confluenced and became the Aire and Calder River, which eventually ran into the River Ouse and went out to sea at Hull. A couple of miles from town was the M62 Motorway, which linked to the M1 and the south and ran east to Hull and west to Lancashire.

The road, rail and river systems were constantly busy, carrying materials into town and carrying produce, including coal, away to the outside world. I say "the outside world" because Cas was a world of its own. A strange type of people, of which I am one, were born and raised in Cas.

With no shortage of employment and dozens and dozens of public houses and workingmen's clubs, Castlefordians worked hard and played hard. Previously one of them, I now had the privilege to be one of a small number tasked to police them.

That I was a local lad was seen as a handicap by some, but to me it was an advantage, I knew the area like the back of my hand, and I defused many a volatile situation by dropping the name of someone's father or brother.

Castleford was ruled by Chief Inspector Gusscott. The mayor thought the place was his, but, sadly, he was wrong, Gussy ruled! Under him were five inspectors, five sergeants, about forty police constables, a detective inspector, two detective sergeants, about eight detective constables, four civilian radio operators, three traffic wardens and two cleaners.

We were all housed downstairs in a red-brick Victorian building, the upstairs of which housed the town courthouse. At the downstairs rear of the building, we had a suite of three cells which were occupied pretty much all of the time.

The police station, better known as Cas Nick, was right in the town centre.

The public were allowed access to the nick via the front door, which led them into the public counter area where a solid wooden bench was provided for their comfort while they whiled away the time waiting for some response to the little bell push they were allowed to use. Overuse of the little bell push usually caused the office man, who was a police constable designated to man the front office, as we called it, to suffer from high blood pressure. When he did respond to the bell, we knew that he was not in the best of moods.

Access to the main body of the nick and the cells was also via the public counter area. Many a time, some little old dear who was reporting her cat missing has been bustled about as a fighting prisoner was hurried past her. At times, some would join in and give the prisoner a jab with their brollies as they passed. Salt of the earth, Castlefordians!

CHAPTER 7

Drunkards

One of the joys of policing is dealing with those people who overindulge in the delights of alcohol, not that I don't enjoy a nice pint or a wee dram myself. I have on many occasions been the worse for overindulging. What most of our town centre revellers did not know, however, was that drinking in excess was not an offence. Making a lot of noise or, conversely, lying still and comatose was.

The skill is in deciding when an offence is actually being committed. Now, ten minutes before the end of your shift at 10 p.m. seems to be the time when the least offences are committed, whereas on a cold windy night on a shift starting at 10 p.m. you can usually find someone committing an offence within the first half hour. And then it is off to the nick with them. They are given free accommodation for a while, usually followed by a verbal caution. Or, if they are really naughty, they might be charged and bailed to court.

If you were the first officer on your shift to make an arrest, then you would be designated as gaoler—a very popular job, especially on cold, rainy nights.

Occasionally there would be a little flurry of violent behaviour inside of a public house. These situations were known as pub fights, and they occurred on most Friday and Saturday nights. In those days, some drinkers used to invite others to have a fight by placing an upturned empty pint glass on the bar in front of them. This was an ancient signal for the bar staff to retreat to safety, for the landlord to ring the police and for the other customers to either drink up and leave or roll their sleeves up. Usually they chose the latter, and off they went.

There are rules and a set order to this form of combat. First comes a volley of beer glasses thrown in no particular direction but done to provide a better fighting surface. There is nothing better than spilled beer and broken glass for a good pub fight. The next volley to come whizzing overhead is the heavy artillery, known normally as tables and chairs, although occasionally a chair will be retained and disassembled to make fighting clubs. The third volley includes fists—again, thrown in no particular direction.

Now, attending a pub fight requires a particular approach. The regulation pace for strolling around your beat is about 2.5 miles per hour. When attending said incident, you decrease that pace to one mile an hour. You also begin to take deep breaths, which you do for two reasons: (1) by slowing down your pace, you are least likely to arrive at the incident during the first two volleys and thereby not present the police uniform too soon, as it tends to give the pub fighters something to aim at; and (2) because deep breathing increases your blood oxygen level and gives you chance to be in a better fighting condition than the revellers, who should by now be getting a little short of breath and less steady on their feet.

You can tell if you have got your approach right when you fling open the door of the premises. It is a good idea at this point to look as mean and as tall as you can, up on tiptoe and pulling an ugly grimace. You go in, identify the worst offenders, ask them to stop being such naughty boys and then show them the way to the nick. No, no, no, you go in and Smackemandnickem.

The best part of a good pub fight is when you return to the premises after closing time to take witness statements from the landlord and bar staff. By this time they will have cleared up the broken glass, etc., righted the tables and replaced the broken furniture with spares—and they will be just having a quiet drink themselves, chatting about the night's events and making comparisons to previous battles.

I learned quite early in my police career that public relations are very, very important. And when a publican offers you some light refreshment, it is not in the best interests of the public or the service that you be so rude as to refuse. And there is nothing to beat a hand-pulled pint of real ale after a lively evening fighting.

CHAPTER 8
Sad Bits

I can't pretend that the job was all fun and mucking about. There were some sad bits, too. One way to see the true tragedy of life is to join the police force.

But despite having to deal with some of the sad bits, there were moments when I suddenly saw the other side of what confronted me. I saw some humour, which was one way of dealing with things that, if not laughed at, would make a person want to cry. And believe me, the public don't want to see a copper blubbering and bawling his eyes out. So, it is stiff upper lip and deal with it!

Death is as common as life, but dealing with it firsthand, and sometimes on a one-to-one basis, is something that every police officer has to come to terms with and handle in as professional manner as he or she can.

One hot summer evening I was called to a sudden death. A poor little old dear had passed away making her tea. I had a quick chat with the family doctor who was present and told me that the circumstances showed no cause for concern. Rather, her age and poor health had brought about the inevitable.

My job was to check for anything untoward at the scene and to arrange for the dead woman's transport to a mortuary, where she would be made ready for a post-mortem examination the next day. It was a busy period, and after a number of severe accidents on the A1 and the M62, the mortuary at Pontefract was full—no room at the inn, as it were. But we had a second mortuary on a local industrial estate that we used in these circumstances. It was currently unoccupied. Off I went to get the key and meet the undertaker there. I turned on the electric, set the temperature of the body fridge and turned on the boiler to provide hot water for the next morning.

The little old dear arrived, and the next procedure was to strip and wash down the corpse before placing it in the fridge.

All done and dusted, as we used to say, it was the end of my shift, and so I went back to the nick to retire from duty. As I was the officer in the case, I had to be back at the mortuary the next morning to greet the pathologist and to assist him in some of the procedures that he had to perform.

The next morning, I took the corpse from the fridge and slid her easily onto the slab. The pathologist looked her over whilst speaking his notes into a tape recorder hung round his neck. Then disaster struck. He made the first incision, and there was a pinging sound as the tip of his scalpel shattered. He was furious. In fact, he advanced towards me with the remains of his instrument, then thought better of it.

I had set the fridge too low and the corpse was frozen solid. So what to do now? Well, we had a cup of coffee and actually talked about defrosting times for turkeys before we decided to postpone the examination until the next day.

I went back to the nick and was met by my shift inspector who asked how the post-mortem had gone. Sheepishly, I explained my mistake, and he called me a pillock. Later that day I got a phone call from the pathologist's female clerk. She had been given his tape recorder with the instruction to type up his notes for the day's examinations, and she rang to ask me if I knew how to spell *YOUSTUPIDPILLOCK*.

One Sunday morning I was doing office duty when the phone rang. It was a rather elderly local doctor who called to tell us that he had been called out the previous night to see a patient who had passed away. She was an elderly lady who lived in a local village with her husband who, I have to say, was rather well-known to every single copper at Cas and beyond. The doctor apologised profusely and revealed that he had pronounced life extinct, left the house and promptly forgot to notify us at 11 p.m. on the Saturday night.

I and a sergeant set off at 9 a.m. to face the complaints of the husband and to try to smooth things out for the doctor.

We weren't given a very warm reception from the husband, who pointed out that we had been very prompt when he had last thrown a table through a pub window, but that we were quite tardy when responding to his wife's demise. I asked him where the missus was, and he grunted, "Upstairs." I left the sergeant to have a cheery chat with him while I went upstairs, where there were only two bedrooms to search. So I was soon back downstairs to ask again where the old lady was. This time her husband grunted, "Front bedroom, pillock." Wondering how he had learnt my new name, I went back up but still saw no sign of her, so I shouted down to the sarge to bring the devoted, grieving husband upstairs to assist me. He opened the wardrobe door to reveal his loved one sitting inside. I enquired as to her strange resting place, to which the bereaved responded, "I wanted to go to bed. You pillocks didn't come, so I shoved her in there."

At times it was heart-warming to deal with such kind, caring members of the public.

CHAPTER 9

Communications Operators

A communications operator (comms op) in our little world was a civilian employee who was attached to a shift and charged with answering the telephones and manning the radio. Initially, communications were done with Pye Pocketfones. These consisted of a receiver, which clipped to your uniform lapel, and a handheld transmitter, which you kept in your pocket. You used your tunic pocket in winter, but when in short-sleeve order in the summer, you carried it in your trouser pocket. The transmitter had a transmit button which activated a spring-loaded antenna of about eight inches in length. You had to be very wary of said antenna. Press the button whilst the transmitter was still in your pocket and you could skewer something you least wanted skewering, unless you were into piercings and such! Press the button when holding the radio near to your face, which you had to do to speak into it, and you skewered either an eye or a nostril.

The other problem with the separate transmitter was a copper's anger! To lose a fleeing prisoner or to have a car fail to stop at a road check was usually sufficient enough to inspire anger, which would mysteriously cause the thing to fly from your hand in the direction of said prisoner or car! Pye Pocketfones didn't bounce or land very well.

Those little radios were soon replaced with a super-duper all-in-one radio called a Burndept. Problem was, they were so heavy that you wore them in a harness strapped to your chest. Within months, every uniformed officer on our force had round shoulders!

In the nick, we had a radio base station staffed by our comms op who manned the radio, telephone and telex machine.

One day we came on duty to find we had a new comms op, which was always good for a few pranks. Better still, it was a shy young woman: all the better to play with!

The first job was for each of us, about nine or ten plus the shift sergeant and shift inspector, to synchronise our watches and then go to separate offices within the nick but away from the comms office. At an appointed time, all of us rang the main switchboard together. The new comms op's panic was instant. What with the lights flashing and buzzers sounding, she was lost and had no idea what to do.

Something you must know about Cas is that the iron content in the colliery spoil heaps around town created many radio black spots which interrupted transmissions. Whilst I was out and about that same day, I made a radio call to Control (the nick) and said, "Alpha Charlie One [my call sign] to Control." I then released the transmit button for a few seconds, pressed it again and said, "Six inch."

The shy little comms op replied with the code for "message not fully received," which is 10.8.

So again I said, "Alpha Charlie One to Control," paused and said, "six inch."

Again the response was, "10.8" This went on for a while until in frustration the comms op blurted over the radio for all to hear, "Alpha Charlie One, I am only getting six inch."

When returning to the nick, I discovered she had learnt my new name as well! She was quite upset at falling for the pranks, so we had a whip-round and presented her with a box of chocolates at the end of her shift. All of us had a laugh and were friends again, but she called me a pillock for years afterwards.

Sometime later we got a male comms op who was a cracker, ex-soldier and ex-miner, but who had a problem. He confused like-sounding words, with often hilarious consequences. He was completely unaware of his slip-ups, which made things so much more amusing for us. One day, his having just being fitted with a new radio base station, I asked him what he thought of the new transmitter microphone, which had changed from a free-standing upright mike to a telephone-type handset with a bar grip for transmitting. His reply was,

"It's much better, I can put it to my ear and get a much better receptacle!"

A motorist driving over the river bridge out of town early one morning saw a man, obviously worse for drinking all night, trying to climb the bridge parapet with the sure intention of throwing himself into the river. Dutifully, the motorist rang 9-9-9 and spoke with our comms op, who immediately transmitted the following radio message: "Alpha Charlie One, can you go directly to the river bridge? There is a man there trying to get his leg over."

I must now tell you about the mysterious telex machine. It was like a huge red typewriter with a flashing light on top. It was connected to a nationwide system of like machines via the telephone system. The telex was reserved for sending and receiving very important messages that could not be sent via the insecure telephone or radio networks. Because time was of the essence when using this machine, you could first type out a message and then "cut" a ticker tape, which was a strip of paper with holes cut in it. Once you finished typing, you could feed the tape back into the machine and transmit the message at high speed.

In the quiet early hours of a certain morning when our comms op was taking his meal break, a tape was cut on the telex and was then transported to our neighbouring division, Pontefract, with instructions that it be transmitted back to Cas on the telex at just after 3 a.m.—which is when our pal would be back from his refreshments.

We all disappeared out onto our respective beats, and after a while our op transmitted a radio message saying that he had received a telex from North Yorkshire Police reporting that a giant condor, a bird of prey, had escaped from a zoo and was seen heading in our direction. He asked for all officers to maintain observations for the bird and also gave a description of said bird.

At 3.30 a.m. I radioed the nick and reported that I was on the town high street, Carlton Street, and was observing a very large bird, black with a white chest and a fifteen-foot wingspan, that had sat itself on top of the Market Hall clock. The op's response was, "We know all about this bird; leave it to me." This was followed by radio silence, so I took a steady walk back to the nick only to be met by our sarge, who informed me that our pal had phoned the zoo, waking the head keeper, to report that the bird had been found.

I crept back out and waited. Ten minutes later I got the radio message, "Alpha Charlie One, you can resume normal patrol. The bird you are watching seems not to be the one we are after."

Occasionally we would receive telex messages of national or regional importance. These were called all-ports warnings, a bit like an APB that you see American cops using on telly. An all-ports warning had to be removed from the telex machine and transmitted straightaway to all radios. Upon receipt of such a call, you stopped what you were doing and recorded the message in your pocketbook.

Following an IRA bomb attack on a military coach on the M62—which sadly killed or injured mostly soldiers' families who were passengers on the coach—a trial was being heard at Wakefield Crown Court, with the accused being a woman called Ward. As a result of the trial, the area was full of known IRA activists and supporters. They were being kept under observations by our Special Branch. The people being watched were mostly using their own Southern Ireland registered vehicles.

If Special Branch lost sight of one of these vehicles, we would receive an all-ports warning. The idea was that the whole force would keep a lookout for it, and it would be picked up again as soon as possible. One night we received such a message, and our pal the comms op passed the following message to all radios. "All-ports warning, all-ports warning, observations are requested for the following vehicle, a red Ford Escort, a red Ford Escort, registered number A-Alpha, I-India, Q . . . er, Q . . . er, A-Alpha, I-India, Q . . . er, Q . . . er, Q-Cucumber!"

CHAPTER 10
Cheeky Bits

In dealing with the public, you also deal with all aspects of life. And with human beings' being what they are, you occasionally find yourself embroiled in what I will politely call the cheeky bits. One night (funny how most of the memorable incidents occurred on night shift) I was assigned to Airedale foot beat. Airedale was comprised mostly of council-owned properties, and—together with neighbouring Ferry Fryston—it was the largest council estate in the north of England. At the time, it was a lively place to live. I know because I lived there from the time I was three years old until I left home to marry at age twenty-one.

In Airedale, dogs walked in pairs for safety, and a cat with a tail was a rarity. It was situated about three miles out of town, uphill all the way. A shortcut along my beat was to walk through the beautiful Queens Park, which in those days was kept unlocked all the time.

I was climbing the grassy hill which led to the football fields. It was pitch-black, away from any street lighting, so I had my torch tucked in my tunic belt, ready if needed. Suddenly I tripped over a large object and, because of the incline, staggered and fell, rolling back down the hill. I lost my torch, radio and helmet. Fortunately, my torch came on as it hit the ground, so I recovered it along with everything else and set off back up the hill to see what had tripped me. I was astounded to find a young couple completely naked and engrossed in the sex act. The amazing thing was that they both had their eyes tightly shut and were completely unaware of my presence. A sixteen-stone, six-foot-one copper had just trampled over them and was now shining a light on them, but they were in a world of their own. I left them to it and went about my business, wondering if I had left a boot mark on the man's bum!

On another night, thieves had entered a farmer's field and had dug up several tons of his potato crop. Marks at the scene showed that there were about four of them and that they had driven a truck right into the field. The offence had been committed during darkness. A chat with a local informant led me to believe they would return the following night. Another PC was allocated to work with me, and the plan was to hide nearby and wait for the thieves to return, at which point we would radio for help and hopefully nab the lot of them, along with their vehicle. The neighbouring field had just been harvested of its cereal crop and the bales of straw were still piled around the field. We found a spot that overlooked the potato field and built a hide using several bales of straw. Once it was completed, we crawled in and settled down to await nightfall and the return of the thieves. What happened next took us completely by surprise. A young couple came into the field and walked directly towards us. Were they lookouts for the Potato Gang? Maybe, so we kept quiet and watched. When they reached us, the young woman removed her jeans and knickers in a flash (excuse the pun); the young man did likewise. Then they both dived onto our hide, which promptly collapsed. It was one big fumble of arms, legs and straw. The look on the faces of the semi-naked couple was a delight to behold. They turned and ran, and when we stopped laughing, we rebuilt the hide and spent a fruitless night watching a peaceful potato field.

Another cheeky story involved a local armed robber who was sentenced to three years. In his absence, his wife decided to use the time to divorce him, which she did. On his release, he found out where she lived, and one evening he got himself drunk and went to visit her. His intentions were amorous. She had retired to her bed and was fast asleep when he broke in the kitchen window and advanced to her bedroom. It was a warm evening, and she had left the bedroom window open. He dived into the bed. She awoke and, with a scream, jumped out of the bedroom window. He changed his mind, ran downstairs and legged it. Fortunately for her, there was a metal porch over the front door, which was beneath her bedroom window, so she had landed on top of the porch and proceeded to scream for help.

A 9-9-9 call was received at the nick. Because I was on mobile beat for that area, the call was logged to me. When I arrived at the scene, the lady still stood on top of the porch wearing a very short, see-through nightie and nothing else. She was terrified, partly because of her rude awakening and partly because she was afraid of heights. I decided not to call the fire brigade, which would have taken quite a while to arrive, because the sides of the porch were fashioned a bit like a ladder. I decided to rescue her myself. First, I talked her into sitting down on the porch and then shuffling on her behind until her legs appeared over the edge. I got her to ease forwards to feel for the first rung with her foot, but she was shaking so much that I had to grab her ankle to steady her until she had both heels on the first rung. Then, instead of stepping down to the next rung, she stepped onto my shoulders, so there I was doing a balancing act with a semi-naked woman standing with her toes facing behind me, on my shoulders. Then the worst thing that could have happened did happen. She lost her footing, her legs went over my shoulders and she fell downwards, causing me to stagger backwards to the floor. There she was, then, sitting slap on my face. We both quickly got to our feet and were greeted by a round of applause from the watching neighbours.

I quickly cleared the glass from the broken window and bundled the woman through it. I shouted that I would return the following evening with a WPC (woman police constable) to take a statement, and I was off like a rocket.

CHAPTER 11

Upper Ranks

It would be remiss of me not to mention some of those chosen ones who were tasked to lead us. The bosses, as we called them—to their faces, anyway—were easy to spot. PCs and sergeants wore blue shirts, they (upper ranks) wore white shirts and badges that revealed their higher ranks, and the very highest ranked wore gold braid around the peaks of their caps, which was an ancient way of symbolising a halo. I found this to be apt, because some of them thought themselves to be gods!

Not all bosses were ogres, but some were, and some liked to fool people into thinking they were ogres. One of this type was Chief Inspector Lloyd Gusscott, a man I am proud to have worked for. He was either Cornish or Devonian, I can't remember which, and he had a devilish sense of humour. Above all, he held a tremendous sense of duty both to the public and also to the police service. Like all other young PCs, I was both terrified by him and in awe of him at the same time. The good thing about fair discipline was that you could trust it. Gussy was one of a kind and always fair.

But he was human and had his little quirks. He hated members of the public who dared to park illegally in his town. He also hated the drivers of heavy goods vehicles who hauled coke from a local coking plant to Ferrybridge Power Station, strewing the road with spilled coke along the way.

Gussy's answer to his parking obsession was to encourage us to use our fixed penalty parking tickets at all times. This was a form of policing I didn't like. If I came across someone committing an offence, I would sooner face the person and report him or her for summons rather than slap a ticket on the windscreen and slope off unseen. One day I was summoned to Gussy's office, where he severely reprimanded me for having the same book of ten tickets, unused for three months. He insisted that I issue all ten in the following seven days, or he would find me something horrible to do for the rest of my working life, something like permanent school crossing patrol on the busiest road in town. He knew I hated school crossings. So I obeyed him and issued all ten tickets by going around the outskirts of town at night looking for cars that either had no road tax or had out-of-date tax discs displayed. All went well until one foggy night, when I found a car with a dodgy disc up a dark side street. I could not see if it was out of date or had been altered, so I was bent over trying to decipher it for quite a while before I gave up, straightened up, turned and walked straight into a lamppost. I knocked myself out. When I recovered, I cursed Gussy and his bloody tickets.

One thing Gussy had us doing was standing behind a bus shelter near to the exit of the coking plant to ambush the drivers of the trucks carrying coke, We had to step out and give the number one traffic signal for them to stop at the very last moment. If they stopped and no coke fell off the trucks, we checked their documents and sent them on their way. If any coke was spilled, we did them for insecure load!

One day Gussy was out on patrol, which was his wont, when he radioed Control and ordered that the Airedale mobile patrol car be dispatched to the top of Sheepwalk Lane where "the road is knee-deep in coke. Get something done." Shortly he called in again. "Tell the Airedale mobile when he has finished at the top of Sheepwalk to go the bottom, where he will find a car parked on the grass verge. I want to know why."

The comms op at the time was a wily old bobby with just a week or two to do before retirement. He could not resist replying to Gussy, "I know why the car is on the grass verge, sir."

Gussy replied, "Oh, why?"

The PC answered, "Can't get on the road for coke, sir."

When Gussy finally left his kingdom of Castleford because he was promoted and posted to the next town, Normanton, we gave him a great send-off with a dinner dance and all. At the do, we presented him with a large tin of yellow paint so that he could paint his own yellow lines!

We did not hold all bosses in such high esteem. One who came later had a habit of checking all of our offence files himself—normally a job for the shift sergeants, but he insisted. He was a stickler for spelling and grammar and would correct our typed reports with his fountain pen, which he kept full of bright green ink. Normally, we would make corrections in pencil so by using Typex correction fluid we could amend the error and rub out the correction. But not with this guy in charge. No, you had to retype the whole page. Great!

One night a PC who must remain nameless used the station spare keys and entered Green Pen's office, took his half-full bottle of ink, and topped it up with battery acid. The next day, Green Pen was seen walking down the corridor in the nick when a small green patch appeared on the breast pocket of his white shirt. It quickly spread as the rubber bulb in his fountain pen dissolved!

Another boss I admired was our shift inspector. He was great, since he led from the front, and everyone respected him. One night (night shift again) after briefing, he asked if anyone wanted a greenhouse! It was an odd question but, it just so happened that he had a plastic and wood greenhouse and was going up market by buying a glass and aluminium one. Trouble was, the new greenhouse was being delivered the following afternoon and he needed to get rid of the old one first. I lived about half a mile away from his house and was fancying a greenhouse myself, so I accepted his offer. "Right," he said, and told half a dozen of us to return to the nick at 3 a.m., when we would transport the greenhouse from his garden to mine. At the appointed time, we all piled into the divisional van and headed off to complete the task. The greenhouse had to be lifted over his fence, no problem; across a grassed area, no problem; across a main road, no problem. But just a minute, there was a problem. As we started to cross the road, the heavens opened and it rained. No problem. Six coppers put the greenhouse down, went inside and picked it up again, and set off to cross the road when a car approached us. It stopped with a screech of brakes, did a three-point turn and drove away at speed. I wonder what the driver thought when he saw a twelve-legged greenhouse crossing the road! Anyway, the greenhouse was transported safely.

There is a story I heard (but cannot verify as true) that sums up some of the police bosses. One summer in the earlier eighties, I think it was, the mixed-race occupants of Chapeltown, Leeds, decided to riot. It was a full-blown riot that got very nasty. I was a member of what was called at the time a PSU (police support unit). We called it the riot squad. Anyway, my PSU was drafted across to join in the merriment. Our opponents raided shops and at times pelted us with the contents of the shops, which initially was not too bad after they looted an off-licence and pelted us with miniature brandies and whiskies. But after they entered the hardware shop, it was chisels, axes and hammers that were smashing into our shields, which was not so good! Then came firebombs—bottles filled with petrol and a lit rag stuffed in the neck—which they hurled at us from somewhere behind the crowds. Then there was the time we were protecting the fire brigade from the mob as they tried to put out a petrol station fire. The pumps and the showroom were well ablaze when a display of car batteries started to explode and we were showered with battery acid. That was not so good, either. The story was that a PSU shield carrier at the front during one of the worst moments went to pieces, lost all self-control, dropped his shield and ran. Eventually he was stopped by a boss who tried to calm him down, reassuring him that he was now safe. Breathlessly, the PC blurted, "I'm sorry, Chief Inspector, but I just lost it. I can't stand anymore. Please don't make me go back."

The boss replied, "Calm down, son, you're safe now. No one will send you back until you are ready. Oh, by the way, I am a chief superintendent, not a chief inspector."

To which the PC replied, "Stuff me. I didn't realise I had run that far!"

CHAPTER 12

Dogs

It's perhaps apt to mention man's best friend straight after discussing the upper ranks. You may believe that the scourge of a postman's life is the domesticated canine. Well, I can now reveal that the little critters don't like coppers, either. One bright summer's day I was crossing fields that lead from one part of my beat to another when I felt a sudden pain in my ankle just above the heel. I looked round to see a cute little Jack Russell scurrying away. I had a neat set of puncture wounds in my leg and, after a visit to my local doctor's surgery, a neat little puncture wound in my backside! Why the dog had run a quarter of a mile across a field with my leg as its target remains a mystery. The other mystery in life is this: Why must a tetanus jab hurt more than a dog bite?

When accidents occur on busy roads, it is not practical to obtain statements from the witnesses at the scene, so names and addresses are collected and the witnesses are advised that a local bobby will call to set up a time to take their statements. I had received a request from a Southern Force to do just this, following an accident on the M1. Off I went one quiet afternoon to visit a female witness who lived on my patch in a bungalow at the end of a neat little cul-de-sac. The rear door of the house had been covered by a conservatory, but I could see into the house and saw someone moving about. I could hear the sound of a washing machine and a Hoover working away. I knocked on the door as loudly as safety would permit, but I couldn't get a response from the occupant, so I decided to move to the front door to try again. As I stepped away from the conservatory, I heard the clinking of a chain and was immobilised as my left leg was suddenly held in a vice-like grip. I looked down to see the biggest Alsatian dog I had ever seen in my life. His choppers were wrapped around my ankle. The dog wasn't biting me but was just holding me. Still, as I tried to pull free, he growled and tightened slightly. He did this every time: I pulled, he tightened. I searched my pockets for sweets or anything that would make him let go, but all I had was a packet of cigarettes. The dog didn't look like a smoker, so they were no good. I kept banging on the door. I shouted and whistled, but to no avail, I even thought of giving the Alsatian a sharp tap on the snout with my truncheon, but then I realised this was not such a good idea, given that my ankle was firmly held in his jaws. I could hear the drone of the washing machine and the vacuum cleaner from inside the bungalow when I came up with a brilliant idea! I radioed our control room, gave them the woman's details, and asked them to check the phone book, ring her and ask her to answer her back door! Problem solved! After about five more minutes, I heard the phone ringing. Success! I was disappointed when she didn't hear it and continued her housework. Control radioed back and said it seemed that the woman was out, as she was not answering her phone. I didn't tell them how I knew they were wrong, and I was smarter than to mention the beast at my ankle. I would never have lived it down. So there was only one thing to do: wait.

After about forty minutes, the contents of the washing machine spun to dryness and the Hoover stopped. It was only a bloody bungalow, after all. The woman entered her kitchen and froze in shock as she saw me outside of her rear door with a big silly grin on my face. Of course she apologised, made me a cup of hot sweet tea—good for shock, she said—sat me down and proceeded to tell me what a wonderful guard dog Rufus was. And so good with children, too! I took her witness statement and left, but not until I gave Rufus a pat and a scratch behind his ears to "make friends." Secretly I was plotting to return at night with a sack full of wild cats or something else as horrible just to wreak revenge on "dear Rufus."

Of course there is good and bad in everyone, and the same applies to dogs. We even had dogs on our side: the police dogs.

Each police dog has his own servant who is known as a police dog handler. These are policemen who are not satisfied with the mundane parts of the job and only want the exciting bits. The dogs live with the handlers day and night, so the two form a close bond. They would kill for each other.

One weekend in nearby Wakefield, a group of lively youths decided to engage in the ancient pastime I mentioned earlier, a pub fight. But things got out of hand and they caused more damage than usual. The bobbies were outnumbered. The fighting spilled out onto the street and was out of control, so there was only one thing to do: call for a police dog. In a public disorder situation, one dog is worth ten bobbies. However, the golden rule was that if dogs were used and a dog made contact with a person's nether regions, then arrests must be made. This justified the need to use the dogs in the first place. Making arrests results in people's being charged and summoned to court. Which in turn means that the officers at the scene are called as witnesses, including the dog handler. In this case, there were several offenders appearing in court, and the dog handler took to the witness box and gave his evidence. At one point, he said that a certain youth had told him to "Eff off or he would kick his effing dog."

The old magistrate looked over his glasses and said to the dog handler, "Constable, are you quite sure the young man said *effing* and not the actual word that young men usually use in this kind of situation?"

The handler replied, "Well, Your Worship, he did actually use the usual word, but I personally am a churchgoer and find that particular word very offensive and strive never to use it myself."

The beak said, "Officer, we are all men of the world and this is a court of law. We need to hear the actual evidence from you, so please give your evidence with the accuracy that is required."

Dog handler: "Very well, Your Worship. The young man said that if I didn't f**k off, he would kick my f**king dog."

Beak: "Thank you, Officer. Now, what happened next?"

To which the dog handler replied, "He kicked my f**king dog, sir."

One handler had tragically lost his dog to illness and was training a new recruit, a very handsome gold-and-white Alsatian. Part of the dog's training was to come out on patrol with us on the town centre during the weekends. I was paired up with the dog man and his trainee. Chatting away, we were making small talk as we stood in a shop doorway with the dog in between us. He was sitting on his haunches, but with his forelegs upright—the dog, not the handler. I asked how the training was going, and it was explained to me that the dog, although very obedient, had a habit that was proving difficult to eradicate. If someone approached the dog from the front whilst he was sitting as he was now, he had a tendency to snap at them.

We were watching the revellers weaving their way past us when every now and then one would spot the dog and say something like, "Aw, cute doggy," and move to pat the dog.

The handler would give an imperceptible tug on his lead, and the dog would growl and just lift his top lip a little, baring his front teeth as if to say, "I am not a cute doggy. Now go away." After a while we spotted the duty inspector walking towards us on the other side of the road. He was not a very popular boss; he was ex-army, but he should never have become ex-! When he levelled with us, he spotted us, did a smart right turn and marched briskly over the road towards us.

The dog handler whispered, "Watch this." What happened next is etched into my memory forever, and I bet the inspector still remembers it, as well. It happened in split second. The duty inspector stopped to attention in front of us and threw up his right arm to salute. Before we had chance to respond, the dog moved forwards slightly and nipped the inspector's testicles. That was it, the deed was done. The inspector hobbled off, whimpering something about his hatred of dogs, with both hands embedded in his crotch. We could barely stand, what with our suppressed giggling. And, I swear this is true, the dog winked!

CHAPTER 13
Court

When dealing with offenders, a copper's job is really to act as a reporting officer to the courts and to give evidence impartially, fairly and without bias in any way. It is more important that we not be personally affected by any perceived lack of punishment the court may mete out. What a load of cobblers who wrote that advice!

Smackemandnickem, drag them kicking and struggling, throw them into the deepest, darkest dungeon, get them to court and then stand and gloat as they are taken away for life. That'll teach 'em for parking on a yellow line, ha ha ha.

Ordinarily we just concerned ourselves with two types of court—magistrate court for lesser offences, and crown court for more serious matters. Our magistrate court was above the nick at Castleford, and our crown court was in nearby Wakefield. Normally, the courtroom was a very serious place, but just now and then a little humour crept in.

Nearby Pontefract had a magistrate court as well, but they had something that we at Castleford lacked: the sleeping magistrate.

The procedure followed in court is as follows. First, the magistrate's clerk will read out the charge, and then the defendant is invited to plead either guilty or not guilty. In the case of a guilty plea, the evidence is read out by the prosecutor, and the defence case is read by the defence solicitor. The magistrate then decides whether the case is proven or not and announces a verdict of guilty or not guilty. If not guilty, then the case is dismissed straight away, but if a guilty decision is made, then the magistrate announces the punishment, up to a maximum of six months in prison. Anything more serious is referred to crown court.

At Pontefract, the format was slightly different. The magistrate's clerk read the charge, the defendant pleads not guilty, the prosecutor started his summary of the evidence and the sleeping magistrate went promptly to sleep. Usually, he woke at the first quiet period, which is when the prosecutor finished his summary of the evidence against the defendant. The magistrate would then suddenly realise that all eyes were now upon him, and in a slightly flustered manner he would announce, "Having heard the full facts of this case, I find the case proven." It would then be pointed out to him that the defence had yet to have its say. He would then mutter something about their getting on with it and close his eyes again! Sadly, this magistrate was retired. They put him out to pasture, only to be greatly missed by all who loved him.

Of course, all magistrates are impartial. It is important that they are to ensure fair trials, etc.

At Castleford, we had a very special woman magistrate whom we all loved and whom the local villains despised. She was a very grand woman with the composure of stone. She made defendants quake with fear with one icy glance, and solicitors trembled at the thought of displeasing her. Out of court, though, she was a pussycat! Every year on the stroke of midnight on Christmas Eve, she appeared at the public counter of the nick and left a beautifully iced and decorated Christmas cake with a little model policeman on top, along the legend, "To my boys in blue, merry Christmas." Impartial? Of course she was! When a colleague and I were assaulted by a drug-crazed maniac, she sentenced that man to two years in prison. "I'll teach you a lesson for hitting my policemen," she announced, but when the magistrate's clerk jumped up and corrected her, pointing out she couldn't hand out such a long sentence, she was most disgruntled!

At one point, a flu epidemic disrupted the crown court system. With half the judges ill, the crown courts were opened on a rota basis, with the remaining judges' sitting in at courts that were not their normal court.

A much respected judge in nearby Leeds was known as the domino judge because he handed out sentences of either three or five years in prison and rarely anything else. Fives and Threes was a well-known dominoes game at that time.

A well-known Leeds crook was caught red-handed on a job in the Wakefield area and was to appear at Wakefield Crown Court on a guilty plea for sentencing. He was brought from the holding cells in the court cellars up the wooden staircase into the dock of Number One Courtroom. As he climbed the stairs, he saw sitting before him the domino judge. The suspect had been hoping for a sentence shorter than three or five years and exclaimed, "Oh, f**k, it's that t**t." Unfortunately, he said it loud enough for the judge to hear, and the judge promptly instructed the dock officers to take him straight back to the cells.

At the end of the day's hearings the judge asked for the Leeds lad to be returned to the dock. This time the defendant was very sheepish, having had a long day in a solitary cell, and he made no further outbursts, so the case went on. At its conclusion, the judge, true to form, sentenced him to three years in prison. As the dock officers were taking the lad down, the judge stopped them and said, "Oh, by the way, I'm giving you one year of extra imprisonment for contempt of court. Now who's a t**t?"

A man found guilty of a series of serious sexual offences was in the dock at Wakefield Crown. It was obvious that the old judge was considering a custodial sentence when he turned to the defendant and asked him if he had anything he wished to say for himself before sentence was passed. The man lifted his head and gazed at the ceiling before uttering, "Beam me up, Scotty."

A wealthy businessman was up before the domino judge for a case of gross indecency. He had employed a top London barrister to defend him. The case was going against the man, and so his barrister advised him to change his plea to guilty, which would enable the barrister to plead for clemency. Everyone was aware of the judge's preference for sentences of either three or five years. The barrister in his mitigation referred to the possibility that the judge may be considering a custodial sentence, and he made a very eloquent speech imploring the judge to consider a sentence of weeks rather than years. Old Domino sat patiently, listening, and when it was time for him to pass sentence, he leaned forwards towards the barrister and said directly to him, "We today are graced with the presence of Mr X.—Queen's Counsel, no less. I was delighted to listen to such a learned speech in mitigation, to such a degree that I am bound to take the barrister's advice when passing sentence. As such, I hope that what I say now will reflect my admiration for him." Turning to the dock, he then said to the defendant, "Due to the seriousness of the offence for which you stand before me, I am bound by decency to consider a long term of imprisonment; however, I must also consider your change of plea, which has saved the court a considerable amount of time—and furthermore, I feel obliged to listen to the advice of your learned counsel. Therefore, I sentence you to one hundred and fifty-six weeks in prison."

CHAPTER 14

Bonkers

In any large town with a reasonably large population, it goes without saying that a percentage of that population will be mentally ill or, as we sympathetically referred to the people who suffered from this condition, bonkers. These people can range from the eccentric to the downright raving loonies. Sadly, the state of bonkersness affects people right across the social scale, as a colleague discovered one pleasant summer's evening. Oh, by the way, late afternoon to dawn is the time for the bonkers to bring attention to themselves.

We had a system of property protection called Holiday Cards. When going away, you could pop into the nick and complete a card—and, if possible, during late afternoon or at night, a bobby would check the security of your property whilst you were away. My colleague had the card for a very grand house occupied by a retired army officer, but the gentleman had failed to notify us of his return from holiday. My mate was walking through the grounds and checking the outbuildings when the old gent saw someone in "dark clothing, acting in a rather suspicious manner. "So I threw the window open and let the bounder have two barrels of birdshot." Fortunately, the gentleman's aim was marred by age or Port (or maybe both), and so he missed. He also missed the chance to keep his shotgun certificate the next time it was up for renewal!

I got a call to check out a man acting strangely on top of a telephone box—you know, the big old red ones. En route, I pondered what could be normal behaviour on top of a phone box. Once I arrived, I was confronted with a middle-aged man sitting on his haunches on top of the phone box. I asked what he was doing. "Well, you would, wouldn't you?" he said in a very matter-of-fact tone. "One and nine, eighteen, eight and one, nine, that's it." I asked him nicely to get down and he said, "One and nine." I decided to try a different tack and ordered him down. His reply was, "No, not till she pays as well. One and nine, eighteen, eight and one, nine."

So now I had a problem: a man who was quite bonkers sitting on a phone box, practising his maths and refusing to get down, with a crowd gathering and people trying to give friendly advice, like, "Knock him off with yer truncheon"; "Shall I throw a brick at him?"; and, "Bet yer daren't call fer fire brigade."

I decided prompt action was needed, so I jumped up, grabbed one of his feet, pulled him off the phone box and whipped him into the privacy of my patrol car. He gave his name but refused his address, saying, "I'll go see her, she'll pay then, cos one and nine, eighteen." Following one of the mandates of the Mental Health Act, which was to take him to a place of safety, my next action was well documented. I took him to the safest place I knew of: the nick. Halfway there, the man climbed into the rear seat and wedged himself up onto the rear parcel shelf. I was struggling to keep the car on the road as he climbed over, but he looked fairly comfy, so I left him as he was and continued to the nick. On arrival, he refused to get down, so I got help to remove him from the car and take him into a detention room, which is a bit friendlier than a cell, but not by much. Calls were made to get a social worker and a doctor to the nick, with a view to detaining the man in a mental hospital under the Mental Health Act, but the social worker knew him. He was already an inmate of a mental home and had run away. So, after a short chat, we decided that he could be returned and handed over to staff at the home. It transpired that he had gone AWOL and was making his way to Buckingham Palace to remonstrate with the Queen because she did not pay vehicle road tax. What the numbers he had been reciting had to do with anything was his business, and he chose not to let us into his secret. We put him back in the patrol car, and he immediately wedged himself on the rear parcel shelf again. On arrival at the loony bin—sorry, mental home—he again refused to get himself out, so a kindly male nurse stuck a needle in his bum, at which point he went all floppy and could be slid out quite easily. I remember thinking it would be handy to have a few of those needles on hand to use on a busy Friday night on the town centre!

Some of the poor unfortunates are worse than others and occasionally try to hurt themselves. One afternoon my sergeant and I were having a steady drive around the council estate when we got a call to attend an address a short distance away where a man was threatening suicide. When we got there, an ambulance was already in attendance, and we could tell from the grins on the ambulance officers' faces that we were in for fun and games. It was a council house of the older type, and the interior layout was familiar to us, but we didn't expect what we saw in the lounge. On the floor was a baby bath half full of water, and standing in the water was a naked man. He had an electrical wire bared of its insulation wrapped around his throat. He held the plug in one hand and an electrical extension in the other and was threatening to plug himself in and end it all. I kept my distance and tried to calm him down, but I realised that my sergeant, who had been standing at my shoulder, had disappeared. Out of my eye corner I saw movement in the kitchen, which turned out to be my sergeant. He had gone around the house, in through the back door and under the sink, and had turned the electric off at the meter. He gave me the thumbs-up, and I bravely stepped forwards, grabbed the man and wrestled the extension lead out of his hand. We put him in the ambulance and off he went. He probably ended up with a needle in his bum, as well!

An elderly gent entered the foyer of the nick one evening, approached the enquiry desk and placed a cardboard shoebox on the counter. He whispered to me whilst glancing repeatedly over his shoulder, "Can you look after this for me, old love, cos I know they are after it?" I gingerly lifted the lid and could see that the box was full of paper money. I called my sergeant to witness whatever happened next, because I could see there was a huge sum of money in that shoebox. I was earning not much more than a hundred pounds a month then, and I didn't want any allegations that money had disappeared. You can't be too careful where money is involved.

I asked the gentleman to watch as we counted the money. "Seven thousand three hundred and fifty-two," he said. When we had counted and recounted it, we learned that he was spot on: seven thousand three hundred and fifty-two pounds in paper money (this was before pound coins came in). There in one lump, in front of my eyes, was about five years' salary! We brought the old chap into the nick and had a chat with him about who he thought was after his money. Without batting an eyelid, he explained in a very lucid manner that the money before us was his life savings, which he kept in his wardrobe for safekeeping! But he had recently discovered that a passage behind the wardrobe led directly to outer space, and he had disturbed some aliens who were rummaging through his wardrobe on more than one occasion. The only thing of value in the wardrobe was his money, so he concluded that they must be after that. He gave a full description of the Martians, and in a whisper he said, "Can't tell what they are saying, though."

Then he gave us a phone number for his son, who lived in the Midlands. We called him, and he promised to visit Dad the next day. We got a local bank manager to pop round and chat with the gentleman about the safety of his money and how it could earn interest in a bank, but he wasn't sure until we convinced him that the bank vault was Martian-proof!

Knottingley on the A1 was a subdivision of Castleford, and, because it was a smaller town, it had a smaller number of police officers. But since the place was only five minutes down the road, we could always supplement their numbers, if required.

Whilst on mobile patrol on the Ferry Fryston Estate, I received a call for assistance from a Knottingley officer who was on a foot patrol on an estate quite close to our boundary. I was nearest, so I was first to arrive to assist him. I could not believe my eyes when I arrived: there in the street was the biggest human being I have ever seen. He was massive, well over six feet tall, and built like the proverbial brick outhouse. He was lumbering back and forth like a lost elephant. Behind him was an ambulance with the rear doors open. Then I noticed the strangest thing: under his right arm he had tucked our distressed policeman, all five-foot-ten of him, looking like a little rag doll flopping backwards and forwards with every turn. It turns out that Johnny was on weekend leave from the mental home and had not been taking his medication. He had assaulted his parents, who had called the police as well as an ambulance to try to return him to the home. Johnny had taken a shine to our colleague and had tried to give him a cuddle and then tucked him under his arm like a teddy bear. The bobby was red-faced with anger and embarrassment and was pleading to be released. Johnny was eventually talked into sitting down in the ambulance "for a rest." The rear doors were shut and we were off. I was sitting opposite Johnny, still trying to calm him and asking him to release my colleague. Johnny just grinned and shook his head. Eventually we arrived at the home and, guess what, that needle was put to work again, My mate was released, but we then had Man Mountain dozing soundly in the back of the ambulance. It took two nurses, two coppers and two ambulance men to carry him out and onto a stretcher. No one was harmed, but my colleague's pride had a huge dent in it. We had a very quiet ride back to Knottingley.

We had one man who flipped his lid and started a siege of his council house home, which tied up all of the shift members for several hours and eventually ended with the house being demolished!

Neighbours had heard crashing, banging and screams coming from the semi-detached house, and so they had made a 9-9-9 call. Our shift inspector and I were first on the scene. On the front garden of the house was a pile of rubble comprised of wood, glass, plaster and bricks. All of the windows and the window frames of the house were missing; we could make these out amongst the rubble. The front door was still in situ, so we knocked on it. As we did so, broken furniture flew through a window and landed on the rubble. We established from neighbours that the house was occupied by a young married couple who had a baby that was just a few weeks old, and also that the husband was armed with a three-foot-long machete or panga. To you and me, this is a bloody big knife! We eventually got a response from the husband to our banging. He politely asked us to go away and to mind our own business. Actually, no, he didn't. I'll let you guess what he said. Anyway, the man was threatening to harm his family and himself if we interfered. We decided the best thing to do for the time being was to stand near the rubble and try to talk to him each time he came near the window to throw out more furniture and rubble. After about an hour, he had started to answer our questions and was crying and sobbing. We managed to slowly step nearer and nearer to the front downstairs window and could see that the interior of the room was missing. By this, I mean not just a bare room, but bare bricks! He had chopped all the plaster from the walls and ceiling, had chopped and pulled up the floorboards, revealing the bare beams, and he had even ripped out the wiring and plumbing! In the corner, his wife was huddled, holding a tiny baby. After what must have now been around two hours of sporadic contact, we were starting to think of trying to climb into the house and overpower him.

There was another officer with us. He was lying on the path at the side of the house, out of sight of the husband but in contact with us, and was relaying our situation reports to everyone else. The inspector came up with the idea for this copper to retreat and find us two dustbin lids which we could use as shields if we had to go in. He retreated, came back with the dustbin lids and rolled them to us. The inspector called him a pillock when he saw that they were plastic dustbin lids—not much use against the weapon our pal was using to strip the house!

Eventually the husband calmed down and came to the window, where he stood and talked to us. Then he agreed that we would enter the house and call an ambulance for him so that he could be looked after. We assured him that we would take care of his wife and child. Once we were inside the house, we saw that the destruction was just incredible. But balanced on the beams in the corner of the living room was a pristine, undamaged television! I asked the husband why he hadn't touched the telly, and he replied, "It's brand new. I couldn't smash that; that would be bonkers."

CHAPTER 15
CID

At Castleford, we had a small criminal investigation department (CID) office—just a handful of defectives and a couple of defective sergeants. Oops, sorry, I meant *detective,* not *defective.* Still, if the cap fits . . . Although I was later to become a detective myself, there was a certain rivalry between uniformed officers and CID officers. They looked down on us, and we looked in the nearest pub for them. They worked in plain clothes for which they received an allowance to purchase. They also received an allowance to purchase "alcoholic beverages for persons likely to give information which could assist the police." I suppose these allowances, although minute, were looked upon by uniform officers as unfair.

The criminal investigation department dealt with the more serious criminal offences. This was in the heady days of old, prior to the Police and Criminal Evidence Act, or PACE for short, which laid out strict rules for the use of detention and interviews as a means to obtain evidence against a person suspected of an offence. Boy, oh, boy, did PACE change things or what! Twelve hours' detention to obtain a confession or release the suspects?

You are joking! Better to arrest them last thing on your last working day before your two days off and leave a note saying that they must not be interviewed until you return to duty two days later. This practise was known as softening. The suspect who was guilty as hell would confess just for the chance to speak to someone.

Another method we used was trickery. It was fashionable then to wear coloured shirts with a white collar. One devoted Catholic lad who worked on a ride on a travelling fair was caught stealing batteries from parked heavy goods lorries. The batteries were quite valuable, so it was thought that his confession was required. It saved time, and when the suspects went to court, they generally pleaded guilty. So a detective sergeant wearing a purple shirt with a white collar put his shirt on back to front and, pretending to be the force chaplain, went into the lad's cell, said a few prayers with him and took his full confession. Of course he included his theft of the batteries in this confession. At court, the detectives dealing with the case denied that the man had been interviewed by a priest!

One evening a large pink rabbit entered a cell and told the occupant that if he didn't confess the following morning, then he, the rabbit, would return the next night and beat him up! There was a fancy dress ball in the town hall that night which was attended by most of the CID. When the lad got to court, he said that he had admitted to the offences he was charged with because he had been afraid of the pink rabbit! Of course, the court believed him . . . not.

A common technique in interviewing was the old good cop, bad cop method in which one officer would appear to be sympathetic and the other aggressive. But what about the sleep method? One evening I was looking for some place to be alone to get on with some paperwork. The interview room, I thought, might be vacant, so I listened at the door. I heard nothing, so I knocked. Nothing. I went in only to find two detectives and the prisoner all fast asleep. That must have been a really interesting case!

A semi-precious metalworking foundry that did copper, brass and bronze castings was being burgled by three men. We had received information of the break-in from an informant. At the scene, a detective in a plain car was keeping observations, and a uniform car with two bobbies was parked out of sight. The men broke through the perimeter fence and were breaking into the warehouse when our team pounced. The thieves tried to hide behind pallets of metal. Our detective was the first to make an arrest, and he took his prisoner to the CID car, sat him in the front seat and handcuffed him through the steering wheel. He then returned to help find the other two suspects, which the officers did. So, with all three thieves nicked and cuffed—a job well done—the police returned to find that the first prisoner had gone—and so had the CID car! The thing to learn from this is when leaving your car unattended, always remove the ignition keys!

The car was found on a nearby estate. The handcuffs were on the floor, neatly cropped in half by bolt cutters.

In yet another situation, a fight broke out between a large group of youths outside of a fish and chips shop late one night after pub closing time. It was a proper brawl with bottles and knives allegedly being used. A call was put out over the radio for all available personnel to attend and quell the fracas. A young detective was in the area, so he was one of the first to arrive. He made an arrest, took his prisoner around the corner and handcuffed his arms around a lamppost. The detective then returned to the fight, where other arrests were being made. You've guessed it: when he returned to the prisoner at the lamppost, he was not there. He had shinned up the lamppost, got his arms over the top of it and escaped. The handcuffs never turned up!

CHAPTER 16

The Front Office

The front office served as the reception desk for the police station. The public counter was also close to the front door of the building. So everyone coming in or going out passed through the front office. Next to the front office was the shift sergeant's office, and there was a glass window connecting the two spaces. One wall of the office was counter, and very impressive it was. From the floor to chest height, it was chipboard and plywood; above that, going up to the ceiling, was armour-plated glass—grenade-proof, we were told. The outer wall of the office was all window with normal glass from just above the floor to ceiling height. Now, think about this. If we came under attack by terrorists, were they going to throw a grenade at the counter glass or the plywood base, or were they just going to stand outside and lob a bomb through the ordinary glass window? Two thousand pounds, we were told, was spent on our protection!

Life in the front office could be slow in the extreme or else extremely busy. A uniform bobby was designated to man the front office each shift, so we were open for business 24/7, as they say now. And you never knew from one minute to the next what was going to come through the door. The majority of the time it seemed to be old ladies who had lost something, or maybe a drunk looking for something, but at other times it could be extremely interesting, like when a gentleman came to the counter to report a murder to me. He was the chief archaeologist for the County Council, and they were doing a dig on the site of the old Whelbeck School, which had been built over a Roman settlement but was now demolished. The site was being checked out before new development began. They had found a round pit about two feet wide and three feet deep which contained a male skeleton in a crouched position with a metal spike through his temple. This was an apparently common means of disposing of a slave who had outlived his usefulness. A quick statement from the archaeologist, a report to the coroner, a sample of the old chap sent for carbon dating, and that was it—a murder enquiry started and finished by a single uniform police constable. A unique occurrence.

In the early hours of one morning, a face appeared above the counter when I was posted there. I hadn't heard the front door open, so the man's sudden presence made me jump. I asked what he wanted. In a very broad accent he said, "Wanna report a rape." I asked who had been raped, and he replied, "I hev." I asked the circumstances of the alleged offence, and he stated, "I met this bloke in tarn an we got pissed, right, an I was walking home wi mi ands in mi pockits an he pulls mi coyt darn an I can't get mi ands out mi pockits an he pulls mi pants darn an he did me." I took him to an interview room and informed my sergeant, who contacted CID and the force medical officer who would be needed to conduct a medical examination of the complainant. I returned to the interview room to find the lad pacing back and forth across the room. I invited him to take a seat and he said, "Sit darn, sit darn, would thy!"

At the time we had an arms amnesty in which members of the public could hand weapons of any kind over the counter at the nick and no questions would be asked. The weapons were destroyed. We got the usual collection of knuckledusters, knifes, catapults, air pistols and rifles, spears, clubs, studded belts, chains with handles on one end, and various martial arts weapons the names of which I don't know. Then a little chap whose flat hat could only just be seen above the counter pushed a cardboard shoebox towards me, saying, "Thought you might like these. Had 'em since the war and don't need 'em now," and then he scuttled through the station door and was off like a whippet. I gingerly opened the lid to find four hand grenades, pins and charges intact—in other words, live hand grenades. I turned to my colleagues to ask for suggestions regarding what to do with them and found myself alone, I could have sworn there were two or three coppers about before! Anyway, the grenades were put in the dog kennels in the backyard, and the bomb disposal unit from Catterick Garrison came and took them away. The big question was: Why had the little old man thought that over the years he had a "need" for live hand grenades? Castleford was not that rough!

A little old lady who lived in a terrace house over the railway behind the nick brought a black-and-white Jack Russell puppy with a string around its neck to the counter one Sunday morning. She had found the dog in her rear garden but was unable to keep it because her Alsatian wanted it for breakfast. She wanted to know if we would we take it. I made an entry in the Found Dog Register, gave the old lass a copy and sent her off to walk home. I took the puppy into the rear yard and was taking the string from round its neck when it made a dash for the kennel's gate and was off before I could catch it. An hour later the little old lady returned and said, "You won't believe this, but I've found another one just the same as the last one. Look!" This time the pooch did not escape!

One spring Sunday morning I was in the front office sitting at the desk reading the Sunday paper; the shift sergeant was at his desk doing likewise. We had contact through the dividing window. I must explain that at this time I was under investigation following a complaint of assault. The allegation was later dropped and I was found to be blameless, but for the meantime I was grounded, which meant I could only work inside the police station. Hence I was doing office duties.

Suddenly the peace was shattered when we heard a roar and saw something flash past the office window. It was obviously someone on a motorbike, and whoever it was, was riding his or her machine on the footpath around the nick. *Whoosh,* it went again, and then again. The sergeant looked over his paper and said, "Bob, sort that out."

I replied, "Sorry, Sarge. Grounded, remember?" Grumbling, he got up, put his tunic and helmet on and went outside. Meanwhile, we were still being surrounded by the motorcyclist. After about five minutes, the front door came crashing open, and then the motorcyclist and the sergeant were rolling about the foyer floor. The motorcyclist was trying to punch the sergeant who was trying to restrain him. I joined in. We subdued the man and got him into the cell area, where he seemed to calm down. Suddenly, he grabbed the sergeant's truncheon strap, pulled it from his pocket, put it across the sergeant's throat, pushed him back against the wall and pushed up, lifting the sergeant from his feet.

Choking, the sergeant spluttered, "Bob, hit him, hit him."

I said, "But, Sarge, one mustn't hit prisoners." His reply was something unprintable, so I thought I had better do something quick. I quickly aimed for the back of the man's shoulder and hit him with my truncheon. He went down like a ton of bricks.

We could now take stock and saw that the man was huge, much bigger than either of us, so we pulled his boots off, removed his belt, quickly checked his pockets for weapons and pulled him into a cell before he came to. It transpired that he was wanted in another part of the county on suspicion of murder! We gave him a caution for breach of the peace and gladly handed him over to the detectives who were after him. Never did find out why he had decided to lay siege to our nick on that quiet Sunday morning!

Just off the town centre lived a man who was well known to us because of his drunken activities and because he committed suicide about three times a month! For the purposes of this story, I shall call him Fred, which is not his real name, of course. But I use an alias for him to protect myself should he still be alive! Needless to say that when it came to ending it all, he was useless.

Fred came rushing in to the nick late one night. He had his chin held high at a funny angle, and through gritted teeth he said to me, "This is it, I've done it this time, I've got about a minute and I am a goner." There was a strange odour about him, so I asked what he had taken this time. He made a gurgling, belching noise and said, "A bottle of carpet cleaner, half a bottle of disinfectant, half a bottle of bleach and a bottle of washing-up liquid—oh, and some paraffin I had under the sink." Trying not to laugh, I grabbed him and whipped him into the gents' toilet. I held him over a sink and made him push his finger down his throat. What a mistake I had made! Fred started to spew thick foam into the sink, which quickly overflowed onto the floor, but he didn't stop. The foam just kept coming and coming until it was inches deep on the floor. He was sent off to hospital in an ambulance, I was sent with mop and bucket to clean the toilet.

Another incident with Fred occurred out on the beat. I was paired up with another officer, so it must have been either a Friday or Saturday night, the only times we were double-manned. We received a call on our radios to say that a man was on the town centre telephones and was speaking to the Samaritans. They were concerned that his threats of suicide were genuine, so they had broken their code of confidentiality to call us. We attended and found Fred still on the phone. He gave us a sheepish grin and said he was sorry. We explained the situation to the Samaritan worker and then sent Fred on his way home with a flea in his ear. Off he went at a steady pace into the night. We followed him for a while until I realised he was not heading home. We quickened our pace to catch him, but he looked over his shoulder and quickened his pace, too. Suddenly, he darted around a corner, and we started to run. At the corner there was no sign of him. We figured that he must have run around the next corner, so we pelted after him. Sure enough, he was down the street and running flat out. We followed and seemed to be gaining on him when we realised he was heading towards the river. He turned a couple more corners and then onto a public footpath that ran alongside the river. We were just a few feet behind him at this point. Fred ran straight to the river and launched himself off the bank. Just in time we made a grab for his raincoat, which was flowing behind him. We each caught one side of the coat, but it had a central vent. With Fred's toes on the concrete parapet and the rest of him suspended over the water, struggling, the coat's central vent started to tear—and when the rip reached the collar, he put his arms behind him and fell out of the coat, leaving us each holding half of it. There was a mighty splash. We looked down to see Fred lying in one inch of water and six inches of mud! He got a night's free accommodation and a verbal caution the next morning, but when we got our breath back, boy, did we laugh. Talk about Keystone Cops!

CHAPTER 17

Burglars

The one thing that drives a uniform copper to keep walking around his beat checking door handles and windows on a cold, miserable night is the knowledge that at any moment, no matter what hour, he or she might just catch a burglar red-handed. It happens, but every copper worth his or her salt would like it to happen every shift. It doesn't work that way, but when a copper does nab a burglar, it makes all the fruitless shifts worthwhile. The worst thing is to come on duty for a night shift and discover that there were burglaries on your own beat the previous night whilst you were working!

Sometimes burglars just give themselves up, or they seem to, at any rate. One very cold, wet night I was taking shelter in Grandways Supermarket's doorway. No one was about, it was around three in the morning and I was having a crafty smoke when something pushed my legs. I nearly fell over. I hadn't noticed that the lowest piece of glass in the door was smashed in. Billy Burglar had smashed the window, entered the supermarket, forced the doors to the tobacco booth and filled his jacket pockets with cigs. Crawling back out, he hadn't noticed me. I had the easiest arrest of my career. As I was handcuffing Billy, the shop alarm went off!

Walking past a newsagent/tobacconist shop one night, I shined my torch through the window in the direction of the glass counter. I could see someone crouched behind it. I went to check the front door and saw a figure dart into the rear storeroom. I radioed for assistance and went round the back to find the rear yard and door secure. I then heard a noise from above and shined my torch at the roof. I could see that about six slate tiles had been moved, and suddenly a head appeared through the hole. Billy Burglar saw me and disappeared back into the attic. I ran to the front of the shop and saw him again behind the counter. Once he caught sight of me, he turned and disappeared again into the storeroom. I went to the back street, and again he appeared through the hole. This carried on another two times before he gave up and sat on the floor behind the counter. Other officers joined me at this time, and we watched all sides of the building while awaiting the shop owner to arrive with his keys.

When the owner arrived, I told him what had happened. He was shocked because he had recently packed the attic space with barbed wire to act as a deterrent against burglars entering from the roof. He unlocked the front door, and I went in and arrested Billy. We took the burglar by patrol car to the nick, where he complained that he had hurt himself wriggling back and forth through the barbed wire. I asked him to strip and saw that his entire body was covered in little puncture wounds. He was offered a trip to Casualty, but he refused. So we dabbed him all over with disinfectant from the first aid cabinet. We then proceeded to search his pockets and complete a detention record prior to putting him in a cell, but he burst into tears. I asked why he had suddenly become remorseful, and he explained between sobs that he had taken a small amount of cash from the till on the shop counter, but when he saw me he panicked and put the money back and started his efforts to escape.

"So why cry now?" I asked.

He replied, "Cos I f**king put three quid of me own in as well." That's what I call being out of pocket!

Some burglars are really unfortunate, like the smash-and-grab burglar who put a brick through the camera shop window. The alarm sounded, and he reached in to grab the most expensive camera when more sheet glass fell and hit his wrist. He gave himself up at the nick and asked for help because his hand was hanging off! Another bright spark was crossing a corrugated roof behind a butcher's shop in an attempt to climb onto the roof of the jeweller's next door. The roof collapsed, and he fell through, landing with a leg on each side of pie making machine. He received crushed testicles for his troubles. I am sure that if he is still around, he is walking funny!

Some burglars are quite successful, though. We were on alert for a man who had been committing armed robberies throughout the north of England. He attacked sub-post offices where the managers lived on the premises. He would break in and then threaten the occupants with violence, forcing them to open their safes. On occasion he had carried out his threats and seriously hurt some people. He was given the nickname Black Panther. In an effort to try to catch him, the police fitted all sub-post offices with alarms that went directly to the police control rooms but that did not sound at the premises. There was one such sub-post office on the outskirts of town in an area that was separated from the town by the river. Access to this area from the town was over a bridge. One night just as half the shift were heading into the nick for a meal break and the other half were just leaving the nick, having already eaten, the sub-post office alarm sounded. We were notified by radio. There was a scramble as the whole shift poured into cars and set off. We crossed the bridge in record time and surrounded the post office. It took several minutes to rouse the postmaster, and several more to check the premises, which were found to be secure. But just as we were leaving, someone noticed a mark on the middle of the front window. It was a glove mark where someone had struck the window hard with the flat of the hand, causing the alarm to trigger. Just then in the distance, we heard the sound of an alarm coming from the direction of the town centre. We made a search of the town and found that a paving slab had been hurled through the plate glass window of a large television shop. A quick search revealed that not one single telly was left in the showroom. What's more, there wasn't a single one left in the rear workshop, either. It was later found nearly forty tellies went, including four that were under repair! We had been cleverly herded over the river by the burglars, who must have watched us cross the bridge and then attacked the telly shop. There must have been a few of them to remove so many tellies so quickly. Remember, in those days tellies were much heavier than they are now.

Now here is a story that didn't happen to me or at Castleford, but it is a cracker, so I'll tell it. And like the best of tales, it is true. Honest!

Two friends of mine from training school, both called Mick, were posted to Huddersfield. They ended up working together on the same shift and had dealt with a man whom they had bailed to court. But the man absconded, not to be found. Eventually he was arrested for a minor offence in Coventry. The two Micks were sent in a patrol car to collect him and escort him back to Huddersfield. They presented themselves at Coventry Central Police Station, signed for the prisoner and set off for home. On the outskirts of Coventry, they became hopelessly lost (no satellite navigation in those days). They found themselves on an industrial estate, around which they drove trying to get their bearings, when they came across a warehouse with its burglar alarm sounding. They could see a smashed door and a hole in the fence, so they handcuffed the prisoner to the frame of the car seat and went to investigate. Shortly, they were joined by a few local police officers and instinctively became part of the effort to surround the building to secure it. They were then joined by a police dog handler who commenced a search. After that, a uniform police inspector arrived. Bosses always turn up last! Just then, the dog handler emerged with two prisoners. They were taken away, and the inspector went around his lads, congratulating them on a job well done. When he got to the two Micks, he frowned and said, "I don't know you two lads. Where are you from?"

To which Mick One said, "Huddersfield, sir, and we got here before your lads." With this, they left, leaving the local lads scratching their heads!

Some burglars are capable of quite spectacular feats. One was disturbed in a shop on the main shopping street. It was the middle of winter and the rooftops were white with a heavy frost. Billy made his escape up onto the shop roof and then proceeded to run, climb and leap from rooftop to rooftop across about thirty shops, most of which had gabled roofs, until he reached a junction. There were no more roofs, so he slid down a drainpipe, only to be met by a copper at the bottom.

Another was a well-known metal thief who burgled premises that stocked, lead, brass, copper, etc. He tripped an alarm. We attended and eventually found our Billy hiding on a warehouse roof. He was arrested. To our astonishment, he had a fractured leg and arm and was wearing plaster casts! With a broken arm and leg, he had climbed onto the roof via a drainpipe and burgled the place. Amazing.

But then we got the stupid ones, too, such as the burglar who dropped his rent book, which had his name and address in it, inside the house he had burgled. Another one who, having burgled a bungalow, stole an amount of jewellery and had disconnected a hi-fi and a video recorder and placed them in a pillowcase. He was ready to leave, noticed the drink cabinet, helped himself to a bottle of spirits, drank it and was found, half asleep on the settee, by the returning householders!

CHAPTER 18

Flood Watch

One of the police duties peculiar to Castleford was the flood watch. The river running through the town centre is the River Aire and Calder. The Aire runs from North Yorkshire through Leeds City Centre, and just upstream of Cas it meets the River Calder, which runs through the Heavy Woollen District and Wakefield. Close to the confluence—what a phrase, eh? Where rivers meet—i.e. the confluence—is the mouth of a canal called the Aire and Calder Navigation. This was built to take boat traffic along the river, bypassing the weir in the town centre. Downstream from Cas and along the river was Ferrybridge and Knottingley and another weir. From this weir downstream, the river was tidal, on its way to meet the River Ouse and the North Sea. (This geography lesson is nearly over.) Built on land in between the river and the canal was a small area of housing—about half a dozen or so rows of terrace houses, mostly two-up two-down. There was some sort of problem with the sewerage and rainwater drainage systems in this area, because if the river was in flood, the canal gates had to be closed or else the drains backed up into the streets and flooded cellars. If the river got higher, then it might overflow its banks, cross a field and pour into the canal. At this point, the area called Lock Lane would really flood, and the road through the area would have to be closed.

If high tides were expected, the river would back up to the weir at Knottingley and higher still. When it backed up to the weir at Castleford, it was normally not a problem, but if we also had heavy rainfall in the catchment areas for the Aire or Calder or both, we did have a problem. We would be notified of the problem by the Water Board, and then we had to make an hourly check on a water level marker board on the side of our bridge, which led to Lock Lane. All readings were relayed to the Water Board, but if the water was at a certain height, then we called the Castleford branch of the Lions Club whose members would turn out and help us distribute sandbags to the occupants of the Lock Lane area. If the water got higher still, we notified the Electricity Board and the Gas Board, who cut services to the area. In this case, the occupants had a couple of feet of water containing a percentage of sewer water; flooded cellars; and no gas or electric. At this point, we contacted the former Women's Royal Volunteer Service. They opened a civil defence building in Airedale and fired up the kitchens, ready to feed people.

The situation usually lasted as long as the rain in the hills continued to fall. We had at our disposal a flat-bottomed boat and a punt. Because the water was not deep enough everywhere, oars and motors couldn't be used—and a punting pole just slipped on the road surface under the water. So, how did we move people from their houses to the river bridge so that they could be bussed to the Civil Defence Centre and be fed? Police power, a short length of rope and two coppers in waders could haul about twelve people at a time. They were taken out and fed and brought back home in relays for as long as the problem lasted. Did anyone become disheartened? No, not one. They were Castlefordians— and, what's more, they were getting free grub!

Thankfully, these floods didn't happen every year, but only when all the elements coincided. And sometimes it was different. If only the Calder flooded and the canal gates were shut tight, the Calder would crash into the opposite bank at the confluence. (I'm liking that word, *confluence.*) The Lock Lane area would not flood, but the fields and road in between Cas and Allerton Bywater would. When the water got high enough, it ran back into the river downstream of the town. At this point, the road would be a torrent and had to be closed to traffic. One afternoon I was sent to close the road and the canal bridge, since the Calder was in flood, the riverbank had collapsed and the road to Allerton Bywater needed to be closed. Colleagues from the next division were closing the road at their side. We were joined by an ambulance and crew. All present were watching the water rapidly deepening and heading for the apex of the bridge. Across the fields we spotted an Austin Mini saloon car half bobbing towards us but going sideways at the same time. We could see that it had left the road and was into the field, and it was nearing the river more quickly than it was getting to us. The ambulance crew decided that a rescue was needed, so off they drove into the water. They broke through a hedge and were better able to drive on the field against the torrent than the Mini was. The crew managed to intercept the car and remove the occupant just before it bobbed off at a quickening pace towards Hull and the North Sea. The ambulance turned and headed back towards us, but after a while the water was deeper and the ambulance started bobbing sideward as well. Quickly, the crew, with the Mini driver in tow, abandoned the ambulance, got into the waist-deep water and managed to wade slowly back to us and safety. Then we realised that the car driver was wearing a cassock and dog collar. He was a vicar from a local village and had been sent by his wife to do some shopping in Cas. He had seen the floods but had decided it was better to face the elements than return to his wife—and face her wrath—empty-handed.

As a footnote, the ambulance was recovered three days later on the very edge of the river, just a couple of feet away from a point where it would have been swept seaward. The Mini was never seen again.

CHAPTER 19

Burglar Alarms

I've already talked about burglars, but what about alarms? Most coppers cringe at the mention of them, as they bring back so many memories of cold, wet, miserable nights spent standing outside of factories, shops, schools or whatever, waiting for keyholders to arrive and then finding the alarm to have been a false one caused by wind, open windows, blowing curtains or—more often than you would expect—cats. Why factories should have cats is beyond me. To keep the mouse population down? What's wrong with mice? They don't activate alarms. Leave the mice alone; that's what I say.

Attending burglar alarms can be extremely boring and uncomfortable, too. On one occasion, an informant told us that a very posh house owned by a local businessman was going to be burgled and stripped of furniture, of everything. An operations plan was drawn up showing the house and gardens and the location of each copper attending, so as to give optimal views of each side of the house. We all had to make ourselves aware of the plan in case the alarm that had been fitted sounded during our shift. Then the house owner announced that he had a skiing holiday booked, which just happened to coincide with our shift's night week.

Sure enough, halfway through the week the alarm sounded. It was a bitterly cold night with flurries of snow interspersed with sleet. It was meal break changeover, time so most of us were in or around the nick. Our inspector was to drive the divisional van, and we all piled in after him. En route, we each picked our position to cover the house. We made the final approach on foot, and, keeping low, maintaining silence and keeping away from the house windows, we all took up our positions. We had synchronised watches, and at a set time the inspector and a couple of coppers who had the keys went in and checked the house. All was OK. Guess what? The family cat had trod on a pressure mat and tripped the alarm. We all piled back into the van, where we realised we were one man down. The inspector called the missing man on the radio. No answer. I had been the last to see him as he disappeared to the rear of the house, so it was out of the van and back to the house for me, to search for a missing copper. This time we could use our torches. As we turned down the side of the house, we saw him. He was standing at attention in the middle of the lawn, but he looked odd—a lot shorter than he normally appeared. About two and a half feet shorter! The person who had drawn up the plan had neglected to show the great big goldfish pond in the middle of the lawn. Our matey had found the pond—was standing in the middle of it, in fact—and was well and truly stuck with both boots in the mud. We found a ladder and managed to drag him out with it. We were all tittering. Well, all except for him, of course!

Sometimes a copper hears alarms before they are received in a control room and relayed back out by radio. These are the times when a copper can catch someone red-handed. A colleague and I were walking around our town beat one night when we heard an alarm from somewhere nearby. We ran towards the sound but weren't quick enough, as someone had attacked the front window of a fancy goods shop, smashing it with a brick. There was no one in sight, but we could see gaps in the displays from which things were obviously missing. We radioed our control and requested that the keyholder be contacted and asked to attend. The reply was that the keyholder lived in Harrogate and it would be at least an hour before he could attend. So we were stuck there for at least an hour with not a lot to do. After a while, my colleague reached into the window and pulled out a kiddie tricycle. He sat on it and began to cycle up and down the road, knees under his chin and uniform cape flying behind him. He looked to be having a good time and was keeping warm at the same time. I got a bit jealous, so next time he passed, I knocked him off and jumped on myself. I was quite a bit taller and heavier than my colleague, and the spokes in the wheels couldn't take anymore and collapsed! We returned the cycle to the display and feigned innocence when the keyholder attended. He told us that two transistor radios were missing, but he was puzzled about how the brick thrown through the window could have damaged the wheels on the tricycle!

Sometimes intruders can be found without the use of alarms. I was walking past a large, well-known High Street store one night in mid-December when I thought I heard someone sneeze. I stood in the shadow in the store's doorway and again heard a sneeze. This time I was sure it was coming from inside the premises, so I stood still. Then I saw someone move between aisles at the rear of the shop floor. I stepped away from the door and radioed for help to surround the store. I also requested that the keyholder be called. A few minutes later, Control informed me that they had got the keyholder's wife, who had told them that the keyholder—the store manager—was already at the premises! I got Control to ring the shop and ask the manager to come to the front of the store and let me in, which he did. He explained that in his cold store were one thousand frozen turkeys he had received that day. It was company policy not to fit alarms to these stores, and the manager was so nervous that a break-in would seriously damage the whole year's takings that he simply couldn't sleep and so had decided to come and sit with his precious charges throughout the night! I wonder what his missus thought of that. Sleeping with cold, dead turkeys was preferable to sleeping beside her!

Chapter 20

Performance Appraisals

Every year on the anniversary of your joining the police force and learning to walk properly and all that, you have your annual appraisal. In your first two years of employment, you're known as a probationary constable. As such, your employment can be terminated at any time. Once your probation is over, there has to be a very good reason—like committing a crime or smacking a senior officer—to finish you. So, appraisal time is when you are most likely to lose your job, because it is the time that you are most likely to smack a senior officer.

Reports are written about your conduct, ability to perform your job, ability to learn, etc. It starts with your shift sergeant's report, and then your shift inspector has his say. Finally you are interviewed by a chief inspector who makes an assessment of your year's progress, your attitude about the job, your character and whether or not you are suitable for promotion or if some remedial instruction is needed to correct any failings you may have.

During this process—remember that it occurs each year—you feel a right tit. You have been to school, had school reports to take home to Mum and Dad, worn the dunce's cap and stood in the corner. Now you are all grown up, you shave and have a wife, mortgage and kids, but your superiors insist on treating you like a little boy.

Each year I received a fairly good appraisal with nothing bad said about the way I did the job. To be honest, this was my only concern. At the end I was asked my opinion on the reports and was asked to sign a form to say I agreed with its content. I had about seven years of service when we got a new chief inspector. He had been with us a couple of months when it was time for my appraisal. In I went to see him. He bade me sit down and proceeded to tear me off a strip. He said I was unruly, ignorant, ill disciplined, untidy in my appearance, disrespectful to my seniors and members of the public, and an all-round disappointment to my shift sergeant and inspector. I sat there absolutely gobsmacked. He asked me if I had anything to say for myself, but I could only make mumbling noises. The chief inspector leaned forward and in a fatherly tone said, "You've only yourself to blame, you know. Now, would you please sign the form, Danny?"

I looked up at him and said, "Er, Bob, Robin, er, I'm not Danny." Danny was a mate on another shift. The chief inspector fumbled with a stack of files and opened another one, this time mine.

We started all over again, and I had glowing reports and recommendations. In conclusion, the inspector stated that he was totally satisfied with me. I signed my appraisal and stood to leave when he said, "Will you ask the next lad to come in, please, Bob?"

I closed the door behind me, and who was standing waiting to go in? Danny. I put my hand on his shoulder and said, "Danny, mate, your day is about to get worse!"

A good friend of mine on another shift had passed his promotion exams which qualified him for promotion to sergeant. All he had to do was wait for selection. Trouble was, he didn't get on very well with some of the senior officers and was not very good at hiding his dislike of them. His appraisal came around. It was decided that in order to improve his chances of promotion, he would be transferred to another division. All seemed to go well apart from the fact that he found his new boss worse than his last one. During his first appraisal at his new posting, things didn't go very well and the boss was quite scathing in his comments. At the conclusion, my mate was asked if he had any comments. He said "Yes, sir. Can I ask you a question off the record and man to man?"

The boss replied, "Yes, go ahead."

He then said, "If I were to call you a bastard, what would you do?"

The boss, taken aback, said, "I would put you on a charge, you would be up before the chief constable and you would be disciplined."

My mate then said, "But what if I just sat here and thought you were a bastard? What would you do?"

The boss replied, "Ah, well, in that case I could do nothing."

The lad then said, "Good, because I think you are a bastard!" The very next day he was posted back to Castleford!

Another old pal of mine had worked his thirty years in the job and could have retired, but he had opted to continue in the service until his fifty-fifth birthday, which was only a year and a half away. Appraisals continued throughout the whole length of service. My old mate went in for his very last appraisal, which was not a particularly good one, and when asked to comment he said, "Well, I'm not unduly worried about what a pillock like you thinks of me anymore. Oh, by the way, I retire tomorrow. Goodbye." What a sweet way to go!

Chapter 21

Fun and Games

As I have already mentioned, the quiet times during the week when the town centre is empty are 1 a.m. to 5 a.m., and it can get boring. But put half a dozen young men together, add a little inventiveness and suddenly you have fun and games!

Asda, the supermarket giant of today, had opened their second store in Castleford. They were the first in the area (as I recall) to use the wire trolleys, and they left these out all night, freely available for our use! We laid out a course that circumnavigated the town centre and included obstacles like the slalom through the market stalls and a cross-country through the Valley Gardens. The finish line was in front of Asda. We split into teams of two, one to sit in the trolley and the other to push. At the halfway point we changed over: the passenger became the pusher. We had a stopwatch so we had to make sure we didn't get a trolley with a wobbly wheel, which would slow you down. We had time trials, news of the event quickly spread to the other shifts and soon we had a league table. It was all very competitive!

Springtime meant early dawns, and early dawns meant that just over the river in the half-light there were dozens of rabbits in the fields. We had minivans at that time, three of them, so—armed with confiscated air weapons from the property store—a-huntin' we would go. Our office man was good with a knife and had been brought up on a farm, so skinning and gutting was no problem for him. The mess room table was covered with newspapers ready for the first batch of rabbits. We had one man driving and one man riding shotgun, and we kept the office man busy for a couple of hours. We all had good fun. Those who liked rabbit had plenty of free meat for the freezer. We dropped a couple rabbits off for the farmer and kept his rabbit population down, so everyone was happy.

One night a colleague and I found a large cardboard box full of spent light bulbs in an alley behind some shops. Nearby was a partly finished shop development that you could get into, with stairs that led to a flat roof over the third floor. From this roof, you could see the end of the main street through the town centre for quite a distance. The box of goodies was carried to the top and placed on the flat roof. I say *goodies* because if you smash a light bulb, it just sounds like tinkling glass, but if you smash a spent light bulb, it makes a very loud popping noise not unlike gunfire. We knew that one of our mates would be leaving the nick soon after his meal break and that he had to walk past us to get to his beat, so we waited. Sure enough, he came along about 3 a.m. We each threw two bulbs, each aimed to land a safe distance behind him. They went off with resounding bangs, just like we wanted. But what happened next was something we didn't expect!

Hearing the gunshots behind him, our mate dived into a recessed shoe shop doorway. He lay flat on his stomach, pulled out his radio and called a 10.13— officer in distress. He gave his location and informed Control that he was under attack; four rounds of what he thought was small arms fire had been fired at him, he said. We were howling with laughter as we watched the scene unfold before our eyes. A patrol car arrived, blue light flashing, then another, then two Road Traffic Patrol cars, and then several coppers on foot. Suddenly we realised two things: first, someone was bound to find the broken glass, and second, we were the only two coppers working who weren't among the crowd. So we ran down the stairs, over the railway and back into the town centre, and then we ran to the scene of the shooting to see if we could assist! We didn't bother with the rest of the bulbs and kept our heads down for a while. But not for long!

We had been having problems with someone's breaking into the Market Hall through the roof and, once inside, burgling individual stalls. The old hall, now demolished, had alarms only on the doors, so our Billy was bypassing them. We had the idea that he was gaining access to the roof via the outdoor market stalls. These were made of wood and had roofs. They were warm and dry on the long winter nights, so they made an ideal spot to sit and have a crafty smoke. At this time, we also had a new shift inspector who was proving to be a bit of a pain. He kept checking up on us, making sure we didn't stray off our beats or slip away for a cuppa somewhere. He would walk round your beat, noting the time, and then later he would ask you where you were at a particular time, always trying to catch you out.

I and the same colleague who was involved in the light bulb incident sat one dark night on the market stalls, keeping warm and having a smoke. There was only one street light on a corner as one entered the stalls, after which point it became very dark. Suddenly we saw our inspector round the corner. As he passed under the light, we could clearly see that it was him. Whispering, we hatched a plan and sunk back into the dark. I unbuttoned my uniform cape and waited. As the inspector passed us, we pounced. I threw my cape over his head and shoulders, and then my colleague and I rugby-tackled him to the ground and roughed him up a little. We got his arms behind him and handcuffed him before we pulled him to his feet, all the time shouting things like, "Keep still," Don't struggle," "We have got you at last," and then we pulled him to the light and removed the cape. We had to pretend we were shocked at finding that we had nicked our own boss. We claimed to have thought we had finally caught the Market Hall burglar. The inspector was not a happy bunny, but, strangely, he stopped creeping around our beats at night!

CHAPTER 22

Traffic Wardens

We had three traffic wardens at Castleford. In their own way, they did a brilliant job. They were hated by most of the public but had an important job to do. It took quite a resilient character to fulfil the tasks these traffic wardens were burdened with.

A traffic warden's job is basically to ensure a free flow of traffic through a town. The way to accomplish this is to enforce the parking regulations. Parking is not allowed in places where a stationary vehicle would impede the flow of traffic or cause a danger to other road users or pedestrians. Also, a traffic warden should be an evil, vindictive, aggressive, perverse, antisocial misfit who hates children. Just thought I'd add that last bit so that I appear impartial!

A heavy goods vehicle was parked on yellow lines with its rear doors open, giving the impression that it was loading or unloading, which it was allowed to do, but only for a certain time. Our traffic warden spotted it and made a note in her little notebook, showing the time, etc. She returned after half an hour to find the vehicle still there with its rear doors still open. She walked around the vehicle; there was no driver in sight. Then she spotted him seated through the window of a café across the street. He was tucking into a full English breakfast and pretending not to watch her. She knew he was the driver of the vehicle because he was wearing an overall that bore a large logo matching the one on the side of the vehicle. The traffic warden made out a ticket and stuck it on the windscreen. The driver shot out of the café and ran over to her, protesting that he was loading from the back door of the nearby supermarket. She pointed out that he had egg yolk on his chin and told him why she had issued the parking fine. He was furious and spluttered, "You want f**cking . . ."

Calmly, the traffic warden turned to the driver, fluttered her eyes and said, "Oh, so you'd like to settle out of court, would you, big boy?"

Another motorist just went just too far. He had parked on double yellow lines while he popped into a shop. The traffic warden came round the corner and popped him a ticket on the windscreen. The motorist came out of the shop and tried to get her to cancel the ticket, but she wasn't having any. In fact, once issued, a ticket couldn't be taken back anyway. The man really lost his cool, grabbed the traffic warden's tunic lapel and pushed the ticket into her jacket. At this point he had committed an assault, but his fingernails caught the side of her breast, causing bruising and scratches. Now it was assault occasioning actual bodily harm, or AOABH for short. She radioed for assistance and the man was arrested.

Now, our traffic warden was a great practical joker and was notorious for teasing young probationary constables, telling them she fancied them and so forth. So now it was her turn. We told her that for evidential purposes we needed to have her injuries photographed by our Scenes of Crime officer. She was reluctant at first, but we convinced her that it was necessary. We then told her that the Scenes of Crime man wanted to avoid any allegations of sexual assault by the traffic warden, so he insisted that another male officer be present whilst the photos were taken. She was puzzled but agreed. The camera was set up in a vacant interview room, and she sat ready to be photographed. She opened her shirt and pulled her bra down until the marks were visible. We told her that this was insufficient and that we had to have a shot of the whole breast, as that was the only way to show the full extent of the injury. So she pulled the bra right down, and we took a photo. Then very matter-of-factly she was asked to expose both breasts. She wanted to know why, so we explained that it was for comparison purposes, to enable the court to see what an undamaged one looked like. She then completely removed her shirt and bra and sat naked to the waist, posing for the last shot. When we said we wanted another shot with one of us holding a ruler across her chest so that size comparisons could be made, the penny dropped. Her language from that point on was not very ladylike! For months afterwards, we teased her by threatening to make copies of the photos and sticking them on lampposts around town.

CHAPTER 23

Juveniles

Kids between the ages of eleven and seventeen are classed as juveniles. They can be complete nuisances, but they can also be very rewarding to work with.

I was once a kid, brought up in the area I was now policing, so all the joys and all the problems these kids were experiencing, I had experienced before them. I had had my lughole clipped by the local copper for riding my pushbike on the pavement. I had been stuck up a pear tree for three hours because the gardener had selfishly decided to dig his orchard whilst I was nicking his pears. I had played hide-and-seek on the school roof. I had pinched six-inch nails from the woodyard, laid them along the railway lines and waited for a train to flatten them into throwing knives. I had followed the rent collector on her rounds and at each house let a bit more air out of her pushbike tyres. I had made banger guns using copper pipe and fireworks. I also made throwing arrows from old stair rods, and catapults to fire at people's heads after the lights went down for Saturday matinee at the local cinema, which we aptly named the Bug and Scratch. When that building was demolished it, millions of lice and cockroaches were left homeless!

So, whatever the kids on my beat got up to, I knew about it. And I also knew where they did their deeds.

One afternoon I walked through a recreation ground which had been seeing a bit of vandalism, as I had promised to do now and again. I noticed a lad of about seventeen sitting in a shelter. He had his hands deep in his pockets and was staring at the ground. "Good morning" got no response, so I walked on. Later that day I passed through again and he was still sitting there, still staring at the ground. "Good afternoon" got no response, so again I walked away. About two or three days later, I was again walking through the grounds and, sure enough, he was still there—same spot, same stare. I sat down in the shelter a few feet from him. "You come here a lot, saw you last week," he sniffed and muttered, "Yeah,".

"You know anything about the damage to the swings?" I asked.

"Yeah, them two little kids, brothers, I think, about two roads down." He indicated a direction with his head, as his hands were still in his pockets.

I said, "Ta," and got up and walked away.

Without looking at him, I said, "See ya." See him again I did, always in the same place, same expression, hands in his pockets. After a while I learnt that he had left school eighteen months prior, had spent a year trying to find work, and then gave up looking. He lived with his mother and grandmother, his father's having left before he was born. He was pretty fed up with life in general and spent every day sitting in this shelter. I devised a cunning plan!

One gloriously sunny afternoon, I approached the shelter, slumped down beside the lad and let out a huge sigh. He asked me what was wrong, so I moaned about work, the weather, the wife, the boss, everything I could think of, until I could sense he was getting fed up with my moaning.

He said, "At least you got a job." I had him. The bait was taken. I just had to strike, set the hook and reel him in.

I turned to him and said, "You could have one, too." Through questions and answers I determined that his grandma had an old ladder. He could find a bucket and cloths at home, and I told him where to buy a wash leather. He was interested, so I suggested he start near to home and ask his neighbours if they would like their windows cleaned at ten bob a house, half a crown a bungalow. I finally saw him smile as he tried to imagine how much money he could make. I made him promise to declare what he was doing at the Unemployment Office and to ask if they could give him any further advice. A few days later I saw him down the road carrying an old wooden ladder and a metal bucket. He had disappeared around the back of a house before I could speak to him, so I left him alone.

About a month later I was walking through the estate, nowhere near where the lad lived, and heard a call. "Oh, Copper, gis a job." There he was up a brand new aluminium ladder with a plastic bucket. He had a grin as big as a banana, "Got a grant and everyfin, gis a couple of munf, an you can come an work for me, if yer still fed up wi being a copper," he shouted.

Cheeky so-and-so! I thought as I walked off.

Another lad I had to deal with had an obsession with motorbikes. He had built a bike out of spare parts and spent his spare time riding around in the local woods. All well and good, but he rode this illegal contraption through the estate to get to the woods. I suspected he had no documents, so I gave him a verbal caution and told him not to do it again. I even suggested that he get a wheelbarrow and use that to transport his machine to the woods. A couple of days later I caught him riding the bike through the streets again, and again I told him off with the warning that if I caught him once more, then I would report him for summons and he would go to court, having already been given a couple of cautions. Two days later, there he was again riding his bike on the road. This time I took him home to report him in the presence of a parent because he was under seventeen. His mother happened to be in and quite distraught upon seeing her lad brought home by a bobby because he was in trouble. I explained the situation to the mother, including the fact that her son had two cautions. I then started to tell them both about the offences he had committed: using a motor vehicle on a road without road tax, without a MOT certificate and without insurance, and also riding a motorcycle on a road without having a driving licence. "Ah," she said, "he has a provisional licence he got when he was sixteen." I asked to see it and explained that if the young man was found guilty of the offences, then a future licence could bare endorsements for those, so I needed the licence number. She then started to search through cupboards and drawers, all the time muttering about how she lost things. Then she announced, "I would do better if I hadn't lost my glasses this morning." I pointed out that they were on top of her head, and she resumed the search, still muttering. Again she stopped and said, "I lose everything, you know." But then she found the licence. As she handed it to me, she said, "I haven't been the same since I lost my husband ten years ago." I looked at the son and he suddenly burst out laughing. That did me. I couldn't control myself. The lad and I had tears running down our faces. I didn't have the heart to summons him, so I gave him another caution and took my leave!

One lad on my beat was really unlucky. Every time I turned a corner, I found him up to mischief, although nothing too serious. I seemed to interrupt him before he did any real damage, so a couple of times I marched him home and told him off in front of his parents. One day his dad took me aside and said he didn't think the lectures were doing any good and that I was wasting my time and his alike. So he said that the next time I caught his son doing wrong, I was to clip his ear and send him home. Not wanting to go against his parents' wishes, I agreed. The next time I found him misbehaving, I gave his lug a flick with my gloves and sent him to report to his dad. After a couple of years, the lad, now growing into a teenager much bigger than his dad, approached me in the street. He was doing no wrong so his ear was safe. He said to me, "Are you fed up of clipping me ear?"

I asked why and he replied, "Well, I'm fed up wi it, so I was thinking I'll start an behave, all right?" I said that that was fine by me and wished him good luck. I never, ever caught him misbehaving again!

Sometimes it can be heartbreaking working with kids. Their troubles are not usually their fault; more often than not, the fault falls on the adults who should be responsible for them. It was a Saturday night when we were called to a disturbance in a town centre pub. In we piled to be met by an unusual sight. All the tables were upright. No chairs were broken and no glass was on the floor! We were met at the door by the landlord, who said, "You're going to have your hands full with this job, lads. Good luck." In the bar there seemed to be two groups of people huddled separately, but there was no fighting. Then we realised that one group was restraining a woman, and the other one was restraining a man! Turned out that they were husband and wife, had come into the town centre for a drink, had started to argue, and then things escalated to full-scale fisticuffs. The wife had been winning, apparently, and the onlookers had intervened to save the husband from serious injury.

With a bit of struggle, we defused the situation. The woman was more violent than the man was. We carted them both off to the nick to sort things out. He was limping and moaning about a pain in his leg. We examined it and found his shin to be very swollen and a funny colour, so he was sent off to the hospital. The word came back that he had a broken leg. She alleged that her hubby had punched her in the face, and that was when she kicked his leg—as well as his testicles, ribs and head! It was decided that both would be arrested and detained for interview, etc. Upon hearing this, she went berserk, saying we couldn't lock her up because she had two young children at home who depended on her.

With a policewoman, I was dispatched to the house to check out the woman's story about the kids. When we got there, the house was dark and quite a few of the windowpanes were smashed or cracked. We tried the door and found it unlocked, so we entered. I tried a light switch that didn't work. I looked in the meter cupboard in the hallway only to find that there was no meter and that the cables had been insulated with Electricity Board seals. The couple's electricity had been cut off, probably for non-payment, but they could still afford to go boozing! Together, the policewoman and I proceeded to search the house. All we found of interest downstairs was the most handsome Alsatian dog. He was in the kitchen, friendly and in very good condition. Everything seemed reasonably tidy, but a quick look in the kitchen cupboards revealed plenty of dog food but nothing at all for human consumption!

We then moved upstairs. It was a different matter there. We could hardly breathe because of the cloying stench of human filth. We first noticed balls of newspaper on the landing and on the toilet floor. Closer inspection revealed that each ball of paper contained human excreta. A pull on the toilet chain revealed that it was not working. We checked one bedroom and found that it contained a bare mattress laid on bare boards, plus a chair covered with a mixture of male and female clothing, obviously the master suite. We then entered the second bedroom, this time to find only a mattress. Lying on the mattress were two naked boys, ages seven and nine. I reached down to wake them and inadvertently stood on the corner of the mattress. It squelched, and urine seeped out onto the bare boards. Both the policewoman and I were distressed by what we were witnessing, but we had to sort out the kids, so it was deep breaths and get on with the job. There would be time enough to weep later.

In police patrol cars, we carried heavy woollen blankets, so we wrapped the kids up in those, put them in the back of the car and took them to the nick. Whilst we were away, the town centre had gone bonkers. Drunks were fighting in lumps. Every cell, detention room and interview room was full. Every bobby on duty was busy. It was bedlam, which was normal for a Friday or Saturday night! The only room not in use was the newly decorated chief inspector's office, the refurbishment's having been completed a day or two before. We sat the kids in the office, and then the policewoman went off to contact the Social Services to deal with the two kiddies. As soon as she left the room, the youngest child started to cry, saying he was thirsty. He asked me for some water, so I told them to sit still and behave whilst I nipped to the kitchen to get him a drink. When I returned just seconds later, the youngest had emptied a bottle of ink on the desk and was making patterns in it with his hands. The elder child had squatted down on the carpet and had done his toilet. Even worse, he had picked up a piece of excreta and had written his name on the flock wallpaper with it!

The parents had to pay a small fine for breach of the peace. The wife got a suspended sentence for assault occasioning actual bodily harm on the husband. The two kids were taken into care and placed in a children's home. I got a telling off from the chief inspector for allowing the despoilment of his lovely office!

CHAPTER 24

Unbelievable Sights

Some things you see as a uniform policeman tend to leave a person speechless. It is a constant source of wonder what some people will get up to.

At the bottom of town on the side of the river was a flour mill renowned for its stone-ground flour. The mill was powered by the river which drove huge stone mill wheels, each about six feet in diameter and over a foot thick. They weighed well over a ton and a half each. Two of these millstones were leaning against the front wall of the mill next to the pavement and the main road. They were used but were kept as an advertising feature.

Just after midnight on a summer's night, I heard a rumbling noise as I walked down the main street in the town centre. I turned, and there in the middle of the road and heading towards me was a millstone followed by a lad who was pushing it. He had his head down and was panting heavily under the enormous strain. It was like watching an event in World's Strongest Man. I stopped him and asked the obvious, "What do you think you are doing?"

The lad was so drunk that I couldn't decipher a word he was saying, apart from, "Sorry, Officer." The amazing thing was that he had pushed the stone over half a mile, mostly uphill! I took his collar and brought him round the stone and made him push it back to where he had taken it. He must have thought that I was going to nick him when he suddenly made a run for it. However, he was so drunk that he was zigzagging all over the road. I could keep up with him at walking pace, so when he reached the boundary of my beat, I left him to find his way home. He had done no damage, and besides, if he was strong enough to push that flipping stone the distance he had, I was not going to tackle him!

Standing in a town centre doorway, I saw a lad on the other side of the road walking in my direction. He was carrying a great big television. You remember how big they used to be. When he drew level with me, he looked across and saw me. I'll never forget what happened next. The lad tried to pull his coat around the telly and started to run. Not only was he unable to hide the telly, but also he couldn't run very fast with it, either. He hadn't the sense to drop the telly and leg it, so in a few yards I had caught up with him and nicked him on suspicion of theft of the telly. He came clean, admitting to breaking into a house just off the town centre—and that he was now off home with his spoils!

A report came in early one morning stating that a huge crashing noise had been heard somewhere on Wheldon Road near to the rugby league ground, which was home to our glorious heroes who were just called Castleford then (the Tigers bit came much later). It was assumed that there had been a road accident. I drove the length of Wheldon Road without seeing any evidence of a crash, so I turned and headed back into town. I was barely past the rugby ground when just down a side street I could see the rear of a JCB digger sitting where the front of a house should have been. Honestly, the huge machine was inside the house, and bricks, window frames and glass were strewn everywhere. The house was a two-up two-down end terrace, and it was in darkness. I scrambled through the rubble past the machine to the foot of the staircase and shouted as loud as I could to see if the house was occupied. There was no answer. Inside the cab of the machine I saw that the rear-view mirror was smashed and had blood and hair on it. Whilst our Scenes of Crime officer was taking samples an hour or so after the time of the initial report, we were startled when a young man came down the stairs to join us! He was rubbing his eyes and yawning, half asleep. He asked us what we were doing and then noticed the digger where his settee used to be. His language was rich, mixed with Anglo-Saxon. He explained that the previous afternoon, he and the lady upstairs had gotten married. They were late getting to sleep and had woken when they heard our voices downstairs. They hadn't heard the machine demolish their lounge wall at all. Must have been some wedding night! Did the Earth move for you?

The house was later shored up, the digger removed and the front of the house rebuilt. The couple had gone on honeymoon the following day, and, with help from the insurance and their relatives, everything was put right before their return. The drunk who had nicked the digger from a building site was found and went for a spell of free meals courtesy of Her Majesty. Nice when you get a happy ending, isn't it?

Standing at the foot of the river bridge five o'clock one morning, tired after a busy night shift, I was taking a breather and watching goldfinches feeding on the riverbank when out of my eye corner I saw something move. I turned to look across the wide road junction when something moved again, but I couldn't see what it was, I rubbed my eyes and thought that maybe I was more tired than I thought. And there it was again, but still nothing to see. Then I realised that the tarmac in the centre of the junction seemed higher than the surrounding area. I rubbed my eyes again and, yes, the road surface was moving! An area about ten feet by three feet was definitely high. Then it moved again, and again. The lump was growing in height whilst I was watching it! It reached about three feet in height. I heard a crunching noise as the tarmac split and a jet of water shot straight towards the sky, much higher than the buildings around the junction, but the pressure immediately dropped and the jet subsided to around head height. The split in the tarmac was quite wide, so a fair amount of water was gushing out and flooding the road. A burst high-pressure water main was the problem. I radioed our control room, and the day shift dealt with the matter. It took the Water Board three days to fix the problem, but what a spectacle I had witnessed.

A family who lived on my beat witnessed a road accident in another county, so I was allocated the request to obtain witness statements from both the husband and wife. He was a collier, and as usual for collier's, his house was piping hot with a coal fire roaring up the fireback. I sat at the dining table and wrote down both statements. At the other end of the through lounge in front of the fire sat a toddler of about two years old. A brown-and-white dog sat on either side of him, and there was a gap about a yard long between each. I finished writing, looked up and stared. One of the dogs had turned around, and I could see now that it was in fact a goat. And then I could see by the firelight that fleas were jumping back and forth between the goat, the child and the dog.

There was a colliery on my beat, and at that colliery were two explosives stores, one near to the pit head where sticks of dynamite were issued to miners who used it underground to blast rock and get at the coal, and another at the bottom of the pit yard, well away from other buildings, where the bulk of the dynamite was stored. The dynamite was transported daily, so only a minimum was kept at the pit head. Being on alert because of one or two IRA bombings, I was expected to make random checks at both stores to see that the explosives were being properly handled and, more important, correctly recorded. As I passed through the pit yard one afternoon, the colliery manager leaned out of his window and called, "Eh, Bob, can you pop up here a minute?" I always enjoyed visiting this manager, as he had proper percolated coffee! On the other side of his office was a window that looked out over the pit village. He stood at this window and was chuckling. I stood beside him. And there across the road we could see a man trying to get a donkey in through the rear door of his house and into his kitchen. The man appeared to be drunk, and the donkey was being stubborn, refusing to move either forwards or backwards once it was halfway through the door. It took twenty minutes before that man managed to get the donkey out of the doorway and back into his rear yard, by which time I had finished my coffee!

CHAPTER 25

Off Duty

At the end of a rough shift, it was always good to get home, hang up the uniform and relax with the family and friends, but once you became a copper, you remained a copper. No one goes up to a painter in a pub and asks how to hold a brush, but as a copper you are always being asked, "Here, you'll know this, you're a policeman" and the favourite; "Here, the other day I was doing thirty-four in a thirty limit, and one of your lot . . ."; or, "Can you be issued with a parking ticket if . . . ?" It's difficult not to be rude sometimes and tell people to sod off. But on the other hand, it states in police regulations that a police officer throughout England, Wales and Northern Ireland can declare himself on duty at any time, should it be necessary. It is also difficult at times to leave the job out of your social life. If two strangers come into your local pub and are huddled by the bar whispering to each other, you can't resist moving closer and trying to listen to what they are saying. Often, people find it easier to tell you things if you are out of uniform, and a lot of information is passed on over a pint glass.

Sometimes you are called upon to resume duty in strange circumstances. I had finished an afternoon shift at Cas when a mate of mine who worked in the next division, Normanton, rang. He was just finishing as well and suggested we have a pint together on the way home. Next door to Normanton's nick was the Black Swan Pub, and right next door to that was the White Swan Pub. We agreed to meet in the Black Swan, as I had to pass there on my way home. After my mate and I had had a couple of pints, the landlord came up to us and said to my mate that the nick was on the phone for him. He returned to me and told me to drink up, we were needed next door. A group of about fifty Hells Angels had descended on the White Swan. There had been an argument amongst them, and then one of them was found stabbed to death in the gents' toilet. Normanton police had arrested everyone in the pub on suspicion of murder, and we were needed to escort the prisoners the few yards from the pub to the nick.

Whilst on duty, I had dealt with a shoplifter who had been caught so many times in his home town of Pontefract, that when he needed a new car radio and speakers, he chanced his luck in Cas, only to be caught by a store detective red-handed when leaving a supermarket, a box containing a radio and a set of speakers tucked under his coat. I charged him with theft, and he was bailed to court in the near future. Two days later I was off duty and shopping in Pontefract. When passing a supermarket I was almost knocked off my feet by a man leaving the store in a hurry. Guess what? It was that man, and he had a bulge under his coat—another boxed set of radio and speakers. So, with my three-year-old son toddling behind, I took the thief to Pontefract Police Station, where he was charged again. When my son and I got home, he announced to his mother that we were late home because he and Daddy had been busy with police work!

Sometimes whilst off duty there are sad bits, as there are when on duty. On a day off, I went with two workmates to spend the day fishing on the River Trent in Nottinghamshire. It was a really nice, sunny day. In the early evening we set off to drive homewards, north on the A1 Trunk Road. About half an hour into our journey, we rounded a long, sweeping bend and found ourselves confronted with a large heavy goods vehicle slewed across the slow lane and partially obstructing the fast lane. We passed slowly and saw that the lorry had collided with a car. There were people on the grass verge. We pulled off the road and ran back, to be met with a scene of carnage. The car, occupied by an elderly couple, had run out of petrol and come to a stop in the slow lane. The lorry driver had rounded the bend and seen the car, but when he braked, his air brakes failed. He collided with the rear of the car at full speed. The elderly man who was driving the car had remained seated in the vehicle while his wife had set off to try to find a petrol station. She had forgotten to take her handbag and so returned to the car to retrieve it. As she was reaching through the window for her handbag, the collision occurred. The elderly driver of the car was sitting on the grass verge. He had a huge cut across his head and was bleeding heavily. One of my colleagues started to give the man first aid whilst another ran back to the bend in the road and started waving at the oncoming traffic to slow down. I went to look for the lorry driver. His cab was empty, but I spotted him about thirty yards away, sitting in the long grass at the top of the verge. I went to him and saw that he was seated next to the elderly lady and was holding her hand. He looked up at me and said, "Please help me, mate, I can't find her pulse." I stood him up and led him back to his lorry. The man was in deep shock. He had not noticed that the poor lady had been decapitated in the collision. Soon we were joined by Road Traffic Police and ambulances, and we continued our journey in silence.

Leaving dos are held when someone you work with is leaving his or her place of employment. Perhaps the person is being promoted and moving to a different division, or maybe someone is leaving the job altogether, usually on retirement. One such do was being held in a pub just next door to the Pontefract nick. A sergeant who was a popular character both at Pontefract and Cas was retiring. Because he was a well-liked man, his do was very well attended. The beer and sandwiches were going down a treat. The old sergeant, who was Scottish, had turned up in full Highland dress. At the back end of the night, the sergeant produced a set of bagpipes and, standing at one end of the room, started warming up to give us a tune. Unseen by anyone, a detective constable removed a soda siphon from the bar, sunk to the floor and crawled through the crowd until he was just behind and below the kilt of the piper. Just as he started his first tune, he got a shot of cold soda in his nether regions. He forgot the pipes and did a jig instead!

They say that crime doesn't pay, which, of course, is true. But without crime, there would be no need for a paid police force, so you could say that crime paid my salary for twenty-two years. And I had a lot of experiences and fun along the way!

The End

ABOUT THE AUTHOR

Robin Whatley was born in Whitwood, a mining village between Castleford and Normanton, West Yorkshire. When he was three, his family moved to live on the Airedale Council Estate, Castleford; conjoined with Ferry Fryston, this was one of the largest council estates in the north of England.

He received a secondary education, attending Airedale Secondary Modern School and Whitwood Technical College.

He is a qualified welder, first working in garages in Pontefract and Glass Houghton as a panel beater/welder, and later working as a plater/welder in Wakefield.

He joined the West Yorkshire Police in the spring of 1973 and retired following a car accident twenty-two years later.

Married with two children and two grandchildren, Robin Whatley is now retired and living on the Algarve in Portugal.